Brazil

Heads and Tales
1965 - 67
Peace Corps

A PEACE CORPS WRITERS BOOK

Contents

Acknowledgments

A special mahalo to Stephen Paulmier without whose generous friendship and application of computer expertise these writings would forever reside in a cardboard box in a dank cellar.

Obrigado for the support and invigorating recollections of past adventures to fellow Volunteers--the lates Jake and Suzanne; Peter, JoAnne, Madalena, Daniel, Mario and Suellen, and Merli among others, and the Brazilians, especially the children, from Quixeramobim to Itequaquecetuba. Special thanks to my wife Moanike'ala Akaka, daughter Ho'oululahui, and grand daughter Keali'ikaho'oneiaina for keeping me on my toes.

Mahalo a todos,

Tomas Belsky

January, 2012

Introduction

Brazilians view the Peace corps (Voluntarios da Paz) from an informed perspective having hosted hundreds of volunteers in our country. Most of these Voluntarios were young and somewhat naive in understanding our culture and history. These young people came with an enthusiasm that is remarkable. The political climate of Brazil when Tomas arrived was responding to the shock of the recent military coup d'etat (1964) engineered by the CIA and oligarchy of Brazil. The coup removed the democratic elected government of Joao Goulart and replaced it with a military dictatorship that brutally repressed workers organizations, intellectuals, artists, students and leaders among the peasantry in the vast regions of the drought stricken Nordeste. For many Brazilians the Peace Corps acted as an instrument of the coup and could never be fully trusted.

Pawns in the geo-political struggle to control the resources of the southern continent (read "Open Veins of Latin America" by Eduardo Galeano) Peace Corps volunteers fought to balance the "Yankee band-aide" mentality with honest individual efforts to become conscious allies in local battles for justice. Such was the interchange between people of the United States of Brazil and the United States of America. Their destinies are linked as important societies in the Western Hemisphere.

This collection of poems, stories, memories and delightful drawings of his experiences in my country touch some of the unique characteristics that make the Brazilian culture recognizable in the global community. It is a joy to see how this artist's abundant talent has been indelibly transformed by his short stay in "Nosso Brasil" (Our Brazil). There is a tide of honesty flowing throughout the collection that inspires one to laugh, cry and wriggle. The artist's role is to channel our experience to empower the change agency we possess. Tomas Belsky fills that role here brilliantly.

Dra. Samuela Clemmins

7/20 1st person singular (x 4) Bildey XII-'11

In mid 2011, I found a mottled plank (discarded cutting board) in my studio. As I was about to toss it, I noticed a pattern to the surface. Following the dots, I found myself – ***Yo I Au Eu*** – four ways of saying the "first person singular," in Spanish, English, Hawaiian and Portuguese. The red was added to give life.

Finding Tomas

Seeming oddly serious
The Old Poet beckoned
So I stepped into his parlor
 took the offered seat
 on a soft-drink crate
 with a floral cushion on top.
"What's up," I asked
In my much improved Portuguese.
He peered into my eyes and
Explained twice
For my benefit
Else I misconstrue.
"You will soon be
once again in your homeland
Where they speak English,
An inefficient language"
"How so" I wondered,
"Unnecessary letters!
Life is hard enough
Without increasing one's burden."
"How so?, prezado Senhor?"
"Take yourself ,Tomas,
Soon you will revert back
to being a 'Thomas,'
And carry an 'H' needlessly
 through life.
Let us relieve you of that 'H'—properly."
"¿Properly?"

"Indeed! It's a poetic ritual
old as starlight,
the poet must travel light
For all artists must travel in light years
    no unnecessary baggage
    no superfluous letters to confuse and encumber."
Sounded perfectly reasonable to me.
He gave me a scrap of paper
And bid me write in large letters T H O M A S
Which I did
    and cut each letter separate
        as asked
He smiled, lit his clay pipe
    and pulled the 'H' from the jumbled letters
    closed the empty space-
and "TOMAS" appeared.
"But what to do with the 'H'?" I dared ask.
He reach into a dark corner
    and a small match box appeared.
From the pipe he puffed out some sweet smoke—
    directly into my face,
Another lungfull upon the 'H' that now lay
Like a corpse ready for the pyre
Upon the dry and hardened mud packed floor.
Paper and twigs were gathered and set ablaze.
The cardboard match box
  containing my 'H'
    was set upon the fire
Much as Julius Caesar had been some years ago

upon that calamitous day.
And while my 'H' was being recycled
    the old man chanted
    and did a few fancy steps
Quite pleased with himself
    for having captured another one—
      For the Muses.
And I been Tomas ever since.

Poverty

Daily desperation
    Spiked ca'atinga
      Fuel for Faith-Fire
and Revolution

Why I Joined

This collection of memories has taken the form of poems and short stories because they have taken a life of their own. Of them I can say that they are based on real events, people and places.

While many volunteers in the Peace Corps admittedly joined to avoid serving in the Vietnam War, mine was not the case, having been classified 4A or some such for my severe myopia. My personal reason for joining was to try to do something that would help those people less fortunate than myself in underdeveloped countries, and of course to satisfy a desire to see something of the world outside of America, New Jersey and California where I had attended college.

The Kennedy presidency was a major inspiration and my wife at the time, Suzanne Inge—a vibrant, red-headed firebrand of a nurse from Santa Cruz, California—enlisted us after hearing a Peace Corps recruiter address her graduating nursing class. We both finished our undergraduate studies in 1965 and had no rigid plans for the immediate future. I had tried earlier to convince Suzanne to join, but she shunned the idea as another of my "crusader rabbit" schemes. Naturally, I was most pleasantly surprised when Suzanne came home and announced she had signed us up for a training program.

We signed up for Latin America because we both had some Spanish under our belts and I had taken several courses in Latin American History, including a course in Brazilian studies. We were assigned to a Brazil training program in Tempe, Arizona. Neither of us had ever flown in an airplane before and started our life as PCV's by arriving late to training, having failed to walk the ramp to get on the plane, thinking perhaps, that the airport itself would fly us to Arizona from San Francisco.

We were as naive concerning the great big modern world as the Brazilian underclass we would be meeting four months later.

First Glimpse of Brazil

From the window to the left
I saw the Eye of God rising
over Guanabara Bay
Great forms of breasts
and thighs emerging
triumphant over darkness
and the wine-red sea
A celebration
in the laughing waters
Rio de Janeiro
Red and gold
everything was so painted
Red and gold
glowing
first glimpse of Rio
from the air.
On the bus to the Peace Corps office
an impromptu rhythm section
Stones in a can
In a rainbow of hands
United
a mighty rhythm make.
And I felt *en casa*.

The Ox and the Priest

Russas, in the State of Ceará in Northeastern Brazil is the largest dwelling place in the Jaguaribe Valley—the largest dry/running river in the world. It was to Russas, in 1965, that the Peace Corps (Voluntarios da Paz) sent Suzanne, a registered nurse, and Thomas Belsky, her husband and an enthusiastic ne'er do well, for their work in health and community development.

Mid-day in the sertao the heat saturates everything. Time has taught all living things beneath that excruciating sun to surrender: birds to the cool shade of the mango trees; lizards into the deeper crevices of the rock pile; dogs vacate the public square and collapse beneath a twisted porch or under a shade providing form, be it a construct of God or man.

As for man himself, him we find invariably horizontal— in a hammock with a toothpick, remembering a last morsel of food or love, or with a book of verses over which he dreams, often reading aloud to the family dog curled in a half circle directly beneath the slow sway of the hammock— much as the *Sertanejos* envision God semi-involved in the affairs of man. If a particular man is doubly blest, he reclines beside an angel that refreshes his lemonade and gently massages the frown from a brow creased with the struggle of gaining the proverbial daily bread.

During this time of blissful domestic tranquility, there is rarely a sound save those God would insist upon to tune the heartstrings of his children: the breeze shifting the foliage— a concerto of sorts with a bass of palms and a vast array of strings and winds stirring in a composition beyond our meager comprehension; the delicate leaves of Jacaranda, or *mamao* (papaya) or the *maracuja* (passion fruit) whose flowers fill the air with the sweet scent of paradise.

On a good day in the Sertao everyone succumbs to the joy of surrender— the *intervalo, siesta*, or mid day break is as natural here as darkness follows sundown. Into just such a peaceable kingdom came anathema one particular typical afternoon. I was gently dozing in the hammock, Suzanne, my firebrand red-headed wife, was in a more profound sleep, thankful for the respite from the culture shock of daily dealings with being a semi-person in the inescapable grasp of *machismo* at the health post.

Poor dear, she enjoyed her dreams so much more since arriving in Brazil—the foreign language had almost silenced her; incomprehensible exclamations in a crippled Portuguese left Suzanne helpless amongst those she longed to help. Her sparkling white nurse's uniform and untamable, fiery red hair coupled with the overt *machismo* of the town doctor were a nasty formula for her time in *Russas.*

The ironic and perhaps most painful part for her was that the *caboclos*— the peasants, loved her. They flooded to the post with babies and children and withered adults—all suffering the deprivations that put flesh on the statistics of poverty and underdevelopment. They came to the health post to consult and touch the *Americana*; and Suzanne gave her heart, information and tears to them, and they felt her concern for their plight, and they came in greater numbers each new day than the day before.

The doctor in charge of the post, a handsome and proud man, solved his dilemma of what he obviously felt was an undermining of his authority—his *machismo*—by giving this brilliant nurse full and exclusive control of the garden and plants that surround the health post. She was presented with a rusted watering can and told to not wear her bright white uniforms to the center again.

She had just gotten word of her "promotion" that very afternoon we speak of. So now she slept a tenser than normal sleep, but a welcomed respite from the agonies of being non-understood, misunderstood and standing out— radically standing out in a sea of brown skin, dark hair and dark eyes— a magnet of focus: red hair, fair freckled skin, amber eyes and a roaring intelligence suppressed behind a tongue that wouldn't obey the mind's racings, and all this in a medieval social order that prized obedience and acceptance above all else in the order of things. So now she slept in her bed, perhaps dreaming of California — Santa Cruz by the sea, and her mother, and I dozed in my hammock with a book of verses spread across my chest, rolling with the easy drift of the hammock. The sun was full high and hot when the spell was broken.

Gently at first I heard a voice amidst the plodding muffled sounds of an ox-cart being drawn over the cobbled streets. The creaking wheels and the sing-song incantations of the driver grew louder as they approached our house. The sound of the wheels stopped; the slow rhythm of the hooves on stone stopped, and the voice grew louder, bolder and rose quickly to an angry curse. I was aroused to the event directly across from our door, and knowing this to be an uncommon disturbance, I ambled to the front window and witnessed a scene that was worthy of a snapshot or two. Grabbing my camera, I stepped out into the oppressive heat.

Already there were a few barefooted urchins gaping at an ox that decided to take a rest—quit pulling the crudely constructed solid wheeled cart, and in so doing had upset the plans of the driver—a man, perhaps thirty-five years of age, who could have been a mere twenty, such being the effect on the physiognomy of those without regular nutrition. He was of spare build, as are so many of these *sertanejos*, and upon his head wore a small brimmed woven palm hat that covered his eyes and laid exaggeration to a longish nose— outstanding for the growth of beard that covered his entire lower face with exception of a pair of pink lips that curled and hurled curses and threats at the huge beast, who, with its legs folded comfortably beneath, gazed ahead, looking neither left nor right, but straight ahead, paying no heed whatsoever to the vituperative of the enraged driver.

The afternoon reverie being broken, observers continued to arrive engulfing the central attraction with the street kids in their ragged semi-attire inching closest to the huge head of the ox whose horns formed a near perfect half circle. The beast refused to move despite pleadings, yells, threats and the snapping of the whip from the driver and a number of supporters in the meandering on-lookers. The whip tasted the ox's hide behind the protruded rib cage time and again, still no movement, not an inch. In frustration the angry driver kicked the monster in the hind parts, ran to the front and grabbing the reins hauled and pulled, straining and cursing the reluctant beast.

It was here that one of the two town priests arrived and moved to the center of action. Padre Segundo, as he was called, was a large, portly, kindly man with a slight limp and a bit of a speech impediment that lingered between a lisp and a stutter. He wore a loose fitting, noticeably wrinkled black robe that seemed to absorb even more of the heat than we of a less godly condition might tolerate. Padre Segundo criticized the bad language of the driver in front of the present women and children; reprimanded him for driving his beast through town during *intervalo* when tradition had it that all God's domain surrendered to the mid-day heat. The poor driver, angry and embarrassed, asked for understanding of his situation, and frustrated, turned from the padre, leaving him to perform his magic, prayer or whatever divine or secular influence he could conjure to raise the stubborn ox.

Now a murmur went through the crowd amidst a low current of tittering and eyes that looked away when the priest's disapproving gaze focused in their direction. The question now became obvious to those gathered— could this representative of God resolve this earthly problem that had disturbed the tranquility of a quarter of the town.

Padre Segundo thought for a moment then moved his rotund body to stand in front of the immobile, stubborn beast of burden. Leaning forward, the padre, his ruddy face circled by the beast's horns, seemed to whisper into the face of the animal —giggles issued from the onlookers causing a few wise cracks and curt scoldings from those bound to defend the Faith even in this ludicrous circumstance.

The padre urged, but the animal refused to stir, blinking its huge, sad eyes and chewing rhythmically on nothing apparent. The crowd became more animated, almost able to forget the heat of the day for the drama unfolding. The black robed vicar sprinkled beads of water that seemed to appear miraculously upon the recalcitrant beast's dusky dome, uttering words of compassion and urgency. In vain, all was to no avail; the bullock stubbornly remained stationary, as if it had reached some predestined conclusion to the afternoon's events.

The padre stood back, stroking his chin and fingering the hem of his garments, beads of sweat formed rolling zigzag down the brow and off the tip of the slightly bulbous nose. "Ca-ca-cast n-not ththy p-earls to the the s-ss-swine," he stammered, and hitching his garments turned resolutely and made off toward the house of the Lord. But the energy of his teeter implied an imminent return.

Kicking, swearing, and the snap of the whip continued amidst several stones hurled at the beast, all failed to dislodge it from the position of repose it had settled into. From amidst the suggestions that were barked from the cacophonous crowd of now well over two score citizens, there stepped forth to where the distraught driver sat under the blazing sun in his patched and re-patched cotton-sack shirt, torn and soaked with the perspiration of futility, a youngish man with the dare-devil impetuosity of inexperience.

Asking and receiving permission from the perplexed driver, the young interloper cautiously approached the hind quarter of the ox and set a crumpled paper directly beneath an opening angle where the hind haunches met the dusty cobblestones. Placing the paper into the crevice, he proceeded to strike a stick match and quickly move it to the paper where it ignited, sending him falling backward grasping onto his leather cap in anticipation of a sudden burst of movement from the subject of all this commotion, disturbance, abuse and comic solemnity.

The fire caught, and the ox's head made a sudden jerk forward; the hind quarter lifted perhaps four inches, but in that precise instant of elevation, the beast's tail swept down into the crevice and caught the ignited paper flinging it out into the street where dazed onlookers guffawed in glee as the defeated young man rose and retreated to his position amongst the ranks of observers amid more cheers and hoots.

The ox, which now had numerous supporters in the gaggle that surrounded it, had immediately re-settled into the position of total rest, one leg having been slightly adjusted for comfort, and the tail, which had undone the fire, switched lazily across its broad backside, perhaps dislodging a fly or two. But the beast was quite serious about not moving, and resettled into position like a mass of concrete poured to stay-put despite repeated pleas, kicks, curses, whip snaps, hurled stones and holy water, unholy water and of course—fire.

Suzanne had joined me by this time and had witnessed the commotion that had disturbed our entire two block area, and despite the blazing heat, she made her way to my side urging me to step farther back from the prostrate animal who was nonchalantly chewing a cud or something.

Now came again Padre Segundo followed by his superior, dressed in flowing white robes—Padre Humberto, the moral authority of the community, whose rest had also been fragmented by the hoots, hollers and curses from the street. The street now was alive with people, horses, goats, a few pigs, numerous chickens and dogs — all the elements that comprise an unexpected gathering in a small town a hundred miles and two hundred years removed from civilization as we know it

The figures of the two padres were a striking contrast to the collection of residents: Padre Humberto was dressed in a flawless white robe with red and gold trim with ornaments dangling from the draped garments; the first padre wore black in contrast and was heavier set in stature, lacking the grace and self confidence that emanated from his superior, who was essential trim, well composed with quick penetrating eyes that twinkled with a sparkle suggesting wit and a ready sense of humor.

Padre Humberto, through presence alone, had quieted the crowd, and, recognizing an opportunity to impart God's wisdom into daily doings of his flock, suggested that the wisest creature amongst all there gathered was the sorry beast of burden that lay there the object of threats, curses and physical abuse. "Furthermore," continued the charismatic emissary of the Lord, "the beast was, in its unreasoned intuition, obeying a natural law— a law of God, much the same as all of you, here gathered, had obeyed that unwritten law when, as is customary in all Brazil, and in all enlightened centers of God's Universe, work ceases, and man and beast alike seek repose and the cool, refreshing comforts of the mid-day *intervalo* or *siesta*. This beast was made to violate this natural law—

God's law- for this sorry individual who owns it. Why
this man could not surrender to the heat of the day as
we all do, to rest and continue in a few hours his
worthy efforts to earn the daily bread, is a secret he
alone knows. But here we are all gathered beneath
this blazing sun, looking at a beast who may in fact be
a messenger from above—a messenger sent to teach
us that there are laws written by man— and there are
laws unwritten, even unspoken, but laws nonetheless
— that resound with the commonsensical clarity only
Nature and Nature's God can prescribe. And so are we
here gathered; should we now all go home and leave
this man, this brother in Christ, with his beast to
resolve their difference in their own good time? Or
shall we draw from this providential occasion a less
than great, but none the less significant victory to the

glory of God and man as the steward of all the earth and the beasts thereon?

I, having been disturbed, and now moved to this pitch of religious oratory and fervor, believe we must proclaim for a victory for God and the Church! As God rules the Universe, so too must man rule the earth; and this beast too, must move to it's master's measure—be it long or short on reason and wit. This ox shall be moved!"

Now the crowd grew silent. All eyes were focused on the glistening, white robed priest as he made his way to the head of the ox. Reaching over to his companion, Padre Segundo, he gathered a few drops of perspiration that were cascading from his underling's face, and deftly transferred them to the brow of the beast with that pert, assuring little snap of the wrist common to the faithful, and, making a circular motion above the animal's head, he whispered some words heard only by the priest and perhaps his unlikely subject. This done, Padre Humberto rose and strode to position himself directly behind the beast where he stopped and indicated with a raised hand for all present to observe, and step back, which was done, but not without steady murmuring and questioning glances all about.

Padre Humberto then bent over and delicately lifted the animals tail in his left hand and gingerly tapping dust from a segment, like a plutocrat might flick the ash from a great cigar, proceeded to place the tail between his teeth where prompt and pronounced pressure was applied. No sooner had we realized what the priest had done than the huge beast rose like a whale rising from the depths of the sea, rose from the dusty street snorting unceremoniously, creating a wave of commotion in its wake. The ox rose, the priests stood majestically, the driver bounced against the sides of the cart as it was dragged by the enraged beast from one side of the street to the other amidst the flurry of scattering onlookers. The panicked driver was again shouting and swearing at the crazed ox, brandishing his whip and futilely trying to gain control of the careening semi-round wheeled cart as down the road, this way and that, it bounded.

The people scattered instantly upon the full realization that the beast had risen; they dove into doorways, climbed into opened windows and scampered up trees. Children screamed and hysterically stumbled in all directions, women crossed themselves repeatedly, and gathering infants and children to their sides, hurriedly made toward whatever safety was available. It was as if a minor apocalyptic event had transpired.

In perhaps one minute all was transposed—dogs barked nipping at the startled beast roaring in all directions and no direction; the crazed driver held on to his cart while trying to gain some control, chickens squawked and scattered, pigs squealed and made way—all was turmoil except—except for Padre Humberto who stood smiling at his handiwork of confusion and resolution.

Padre Segundo nodded approvingly and surveyed the site of the miracle. Amazingly, I thought, no one was trampled, run over, mauled, or otherwise mutilated in the melee. Suzanne and I made our way into the house, hurriedly bolted the door and ran to the window to see the ox and cart zigzag down the street, roar across an empty lot and hurtle itself into an alleyway where it was lost from sight. Padre Humberto and his assistant smiled at each other and tapping dust from their garments turned and made their way slowly, but with a certain confident finality, back to the rectory behind the church.

I turned to Suzanne who had a smile wrapped in disbelief covering her entire person. "God works in mysterious ways doesn't he, Crusader Rabbit?" she jibed at me as I resettled into my hammock. "He sho' nuff do, my luv, he sho nuff do. Now how bout some of that lemonade for the man of the house," I smiled back.

July/August, 2001
Todo direitos reservados pelo Amor de Deus

Lembrança do Brasil

If you beat the cock's crow to the market
You may find an egg
I found two
But one fell through the newspaper wrapping
And settled there
Sunny side up on the market floor
As I stood momentarily stunned
Wondering what to do
A thin muscled hand swooped down
And in one swift, smooth movement
Scooped and deposited the egg
Between smiling bearded lips
My lesson punctuated
There stood I
One wink wiser.

Literatura de Cordel (Stories on a String)

The following is a loose adaptation of a folk poem from the Northeastern section of Brazil, a region rich in culture and traditions that reflect the harsh life of those who dwell in this periodically drought stricken area. Conditions, I am told, are much improved in the Sertao (sir-toun) these days, but when I was there, in the mid sixties, it was very much a semi-feudal state with vast poverty and illiteracy. This story is taken from Violeiros do Norte, a collection with commentaries by Leonardo Mota. These poems, literatura de cordel are printed with

*exquisite block prints, displayed hanging from a cord, and sold
and sung in marketplaces and public houses by traveling
repentistas—artists/poets— throughout Northeastern Brazil
and wherever the Sertanejos dwell. To the semi-literate masses
these poets are news reporters, entertainers and barometers of
social conditions. In translating I have tried to maintain the
rhythm as well as the narrative which suggests a bit of the
attitude, sense of humor and values of the Nordestino.*

Lobo Domesticus

There's a story that's told in the backlands
a land where the poet is king
that sings of a most clever padre
who some say did a questionable thing
when he buried the courtly dog Lobo
whose sovereign was a Lord of England.
The wealthy Englishman loved his dog
Lobo Domesticus was it's name
he was fast, he was fierce, and fastidious
this dog of the Englishman.
But he died, this best friend called Lobo
Master's senses were stricken down,
"I must see my good doggie buried," he wailed,
"If it costs me my last million."
He took himself in torment
to his neighborhood preacher man
"My Lobo Domesticus has left me," he whined
"I'm a sad and lonesome Sam,
The buzzards must not dine on my best friend's bones

God knows I loved him like a son."
"Did your dog leave you any money?"
interrupted the holy one,
"If not, I fear it's out of my realm
and nothing can be done."
"I must bury my dog with full honors, your grace,"
the agonized Englishman said —
But the priest rose in fury
and mocked the hound's glory:
"Your fancy dumb dog has dropped dead,
do you think you are in England?
this is sacrilege, what you just said!"
"I'll spend thousands of crowns for my Lobo,"
master muttered with grief bowed head,
"Don't let them buzzards get me!"
Last words good Lobo's eyes said.
So before my best friend left me
a last will we properly drew forth
"FOUR THOUSAND GOLD CROWNS for the padre!"
The English man groaned
And the vicar passed out with a cough.
"O poor doggie, good doggie," pined the preacher
upon regaining his wits,
"What caused your untimely death?
such a noble, intelligent creature you are
to remember God's humble servant,
What an honorable sentiment.
Be assured, my friend, that the money you leave
will be FOUR THOUSAND GOLD CROWNS

Divinely well spent.
Take the deceased's remains to the cemetery
where I shall anoint and lay the noble form down.
If you don't mind, I'll have the money now
Before Lobo's carcass hit's the ground.
He was faithful, and true and wise as you rave,
but a dog is a dog and a tough soul to save."

And so the dead dog had his burial
the money was paid up out front
It was one helluva best friend's funeral
with a mass barked in tongues long defunct.
All the frills and reverential dainties
were grandly displayed on the hearse
that dog was interred better'n most folks dare dream
which stirred up both scandal and curse.
It was soon brought to the ear of the bishop
just what his underling had done
In righteous indignity his holiness raged,
"Was this blasphemous deed done in fun?
In the name of the church of the highflyingfather
and his sacrificed everloving Son,
they held high-holy mass for a dog in MY church
and by God something now must be done!"
The bishop called forth his vicar
neatly pressed his shepherd appeared.
"My orders, your holiness," said the preacher
"your every wish is indeed my desire."
"Well then, what hound of a dog have you buried

in the custom of a cultured soul?
Answer well, thou unchaste beast of burden
else mortal sin shall commence its foul toll."
"Twas a dog of distinguished personage, your grace,
with birth papers properly in place
intelligent and noble as its master—
a credit to the English race.
And before he left our earthly plane
he dreamed of saintly things
and cared to leave a token or two
for those yet to pass through the wings.
So he thought of God, of the church and granted
TWO THOUSAND GOLD CROWNS just for YOU!
TWO THOUSAND GOLD CROWNS
for the bishop, thought I
what else could a good vicar do?
If I be wrong, your worship, I'll dine on my shoe."
"TWO THOUSAND GOLD CROWNS!" smiled the bishop
"Well done, quite well done, good padre
You're a very good shepherd tis clear
you may with God's blessing be going now,
I shant bother you anymore,
tis clear to me that this canine dog
Lobo Domesticus as he was called
was a sterling example in evolution
what a shame his life was cut short
but in faith we all must answer
sooner or later
all doggies are called to His court."

"Peace to you, most holy excellencia,"
the good vicar waved as he left,
"Gilded truth has united our claim
God's on his throne well contented
with Lobo Domesticus at His side once again."
There is lesson and moral to this story
there is substance to this pill!
In death, dogs too may be buried
'neath the sacred and holy grail,
If in life they embrace English civility
and draw up at death's door proper will.

"Don't let dem buzzards get me ..."

Fortaleza

In our second year, 1966, we were transferred to Fortaleza, the capital of the State of Ceará, a colorful, coastal city of some 200,000 residents. The change was most satisfying: beautiful beaches, markets and stores and hopefully less of the demented *machismo* that permeates the *sertao*.

Here we got to see the transformed, destitute peasants of the interior in the big city they had envisioned as the sanctuary from the exploitation of the *coronels* and their brutal honchos. Their fantasies of employment, health care and education for their young were at best partially met.

Most would not starve to death as was feared in the backlands, but living conditions were crude and unsanitary. Thousands were crowded into unsafe, unhealthy make-shift houses that surround cities of developing countries world-wide.

Pirambú, where we were assigned, was the largest favela of Fortaleza. We were among the few of our community that had an outhouse and occasional Russian-roulette electricity; water was carried in five gallon jugs or cans from a pump on the main cobble-stone street.

At dawn each day the beautiful beach, which we could see from our window, was dotted with naked behinds carrying out bodily functions. No one bathed at the smooth, sandy beach in Pirambú.

Silk screen print done in a workshop I conducted in Pirambú.
The poorest of the poor lived in shacks along the beach. This
print is from a volunteer who sent me a copy of the original she
owns. It had been long forgotten.

Literatura de Cordel

Antonio

Antonio came to my door
one evening at dusk
my age, marginalized
tears in his eyes
¿Begging for bread?
—No!
Although he would accept it
were it God's will.
He asked for work
work of any kind
that would feed his seven year old daughter
his wife and mother.
They waited
pressed hard to their mud-packed floor.
I gave the bread
and we went our waysze
feeling a little better
But not much.

Chico

The last time I saw Chico
he was orchestrating
three paintings
pointing and pushing
compositions and color alterations
as his wives
and daughters ran around
the elaborated shack
carrying out the heavy work
warming a yellow
adding dots and swirls
as the maestro mandated
making cup after cup
of *cafezinho*
(six or eight sugars?)
for the pair of portly
neckties
sweating, smoking, smiling
waiting for Chico.

Francisco "Chico" Silva was a folk artist from the Amazon region of Brazil. He had migrated south and lived in Pirambú, a marginalized district of Fortaleza. Chico carved out a place for himself in the international market for unschooled (naive) artists. He painted dreams and fantasy critters from his early years in the Amazon jungle. We spent several delightful hours sketching in the neighborhood. Chico insisted I was an Artist before I had a clue.

Francisco "Chico" Silva, Tempra on canvas, 1974 Collection of Moanike'ala

Marriage Counselling 101

After She Left me
I felt the bottom fall out
Jake was there to steady me
and we were off to the zona.
No man ever needed Freedom more
and I knew it would come
but the bottom fell out
on the moments of bliss we'd spent
together
in our Springtime
well matched branches on a tree
seeking the light
from different angles.
We agreed on separation.
She got the broken second hand
chest of drawers;
I took the kids that weren't
Fortaleza was the perfect place
to get over a failed marriage
Jake was a perfect marriage counsellor.
He kept me from the usual depression
and hyper self-criticism.
We decided to overwhelm our sorrows
with an ocean of good times.
The abandoned cabaret
on the beach
proved perfect.

Pipa de Paz — Peace Pipe

Foremost among the many important doctrines preached by the Peace Corps training staff was the necessity to respect host national values; it was reiterated and pounded into our young , idealistic minds that we volunteers were to never insult or refuse the hospitality offered by our hosts. To me, this made perfect sense — civilized behavior mandated such sensitivity.

For the first year in Brazil, I had numerous "novel experiences" of exotic tastes in foods whose origins were an enigma – but the locals were eating it, and so did I. And the theory bore fruit; I was welcomed into an extended family of Brazilians who taught me nuances of the language (there are twenty four definitions for the word *"manga"*—the hairpin curve in a road, the fruit, the reprimand, the etc, etc.). Nevertheless, I felt comfortable in the *Nordeste* (Northeast) before I could really communicate in the tongue.

One Friday night in Fortaleza, after most of the party had cleared out, I was sitting in a cane whiskey fog contemplating the full moon and the glowing white caps intersperse between the *jangadas* (fishing rafts) scattered above the high water mark on the beach. Solitary figures walked the beach; occasional couples could be seen embracing in the tropical night and here and there small groups were gathered in circles singing, laughing and talking story.

I was drawn into one such group by my *companeira* of the night who was too lovely to refuse. We were immediately on the receiving end of a small corn cob pipe oozing sweet smoke. My hostess winked at me and inhaled the aromatic cloud, rolled her eyes and then closed them, leaned over toward me, smiled and whispered , *"Pipa de Paz"* — Peace Pipe. A mild roll of laughter went through the gathering as I took the *pipa* in hand. Being the only non-local and an *Americano*, I was the focus of all eyes. My Peace Corps indoctrination came back to me—how could a *Voluntario de Paz* refuse a gesture of peace. There was only merriment in the air. I was duty bound to carry on as my host nationals invited. So I took my turn inhaling the thick aromatic smoke from the *Pipa de Paz*, although I had totally quit smoking when my wife had thrown in the towel and returned to America some few months previous. The smoke was smooth and pungent but seemed to have no effect on my slightly booze besotted head. Joking and laughter resumed and the *pipa de paz* made the rounds again and again. Some confusion arose when it wasn't clear in which direction the pipe was moving. Time too became disjointed in the confusion and minutes seemed eternal, but laughter and camaraderie were in the air we breathed.

Then there was a lull, a total silence in which we could hear the waves finger the shore. As I looked at my *companeira*, one of the young men jumped into the middle of the circle and seemed possessed or taken by a seizure as he made weird slightly familiar sounds and began moving about with exaggerated hand and leg thrusts. Now the hilarity became boundless; a few fell to the sand in the helplessness of laughter. The contagion was complete. All were bent over, seemingly consumed and out of control. My *companeira*, fully convulsed herself, leaned over and told me that the fellow, stage center, was imitating an *Americano* in speech and manner. I thought the lampoon was excellent and tried to say something to complement the comic, but the situation intensified; the laughter grew louder and wilder and spread beyond our little circle. Immediately, others in the vicinity were drawn toward us.

My companion, having far more experience and wisdom in these matters than I, gently took my hand and led me off beyond the lighthouse into the darkness of the soft, warm, tropical night.

The Girl from Fortaleza, six color block print, 1970

Liquinha

we laughed so well together
falling through the flowers
one does not forget.

Iraci

She was almost too beautiful to be real, certainly too beautiful to be from Pirambú. But Iraci was raised in Pirambú and grew up smart enough to realize early that she was from the servant side of town; and she learned too, from aunties, perhaps as lovely as she, that bosses and masters cannot resist temptations of corporal dalliances, especially if said adventures were hosted by extraordinary beauty and carefree indulgences.

This aspect of life was as real and impressed upon Iraci's young mind as the hunger that lingers in the belly of the poor, and the hurt of a parent unable to feed a child. This was Iraci's primary education.

Now here she comes, stepping lively, resolutely, yet lightly, over the sand filled cobble stone street in front of the sparkling white church where I happened to be, about to discuss with the favela priest my observations of what he had called "Communist employees" at the hammock cooperative we were organizing in the community. And here comes Iraci, fresh off the bus from Recife, big dream city to the south, where she made more money in a night than her auntie and mother made in the caju fruit cannery in two months.

The cannery work left scars on the arms of every young woman who worked the production line; scars from the juice of the nut that reportedly was also used as an explosive. But here comes this Iraci —no scars on her arms— her dress bright, clean, smart.

Directly to my front, she stops, smiles and asks me in stilted English if I was an *Americano*. Slipping in and out of Portuguese and English, she explained how she needed some help on paper work in applying for a visa to go to America with her *"namorado"* (boyfriend) in the U.S. Navy. He had promised to take her to "Denver in Colorado" where they would marry and leave Pirambú and Brazil, and poverty behind—far, far behind —when she is up there in America do Norte.

As we spoke I recognized that this was a lady on a mission, and also that there was a certain edge, a tension to her persona. I volunteered to help her that very evening when we would go to meet the gang at the *Caixa Preta* (Black Box) across town to discuss her needs. What the hell, I reasoned, wasn't this what Peace Corps was all about—helping host nationals wherever we can? Should I reject Iraci's pleas because she was a stunning beauty?

I picked her up later that afternoon in the Peace Corps jeep I had use of for a few days while gathering fifty kilo sacks of cotton thread for the rede (hammock) co-operative. We wove our way through the noisy, crowded capital to the depressed *Farol* (lighthouse) district.

Directly across town from Pirambú, *Farol* was another story. Ten years prior to my arrival, Pirambú too had

been one helluva mess with no electricity and no
sewage, few pumps for water, and hundreds,
thousands of people — *caboclos* and *matutus* —
illiterate, medieval serfs from the interior, the region
that first struck me as a time warp — a throw-back as
in the diaries of William Byrd and his gang of 18th
Century Virginians. But the *sertao* was real and
reeling from the devastating drought of the early
sixties.

The dispossessed from the backlands came flooding
into the capital. They came on horseback, in ox-drawn
carts, on trains, by truck and by car, by bicycle and by
mule, and yes, many walked and some even crawled
on their knees across vast regions of the state, north
and east to the florid coast, praying as they inched
along: "God grant me this and I will walk on my knees
and fondle rosaries across these 150 kilometers, from
the backwards, long suffering interior *sertao* (semi
desert) of Ceará to Fortaleza, the capital, where
employment and water are plentiful, where there is no
exploitation and there are schools."

So they dreamed and so they flooded into Pirambú,
the southern flank of Fortaleza, and they brought with
them their secrets, their dreams, pains and pleasures.
The poets came and the scholars came, but mostly the
poor, landless, illiterate laborers with their shabby
cotton sacks full of dreams, illusions and aspirations.

Iraci was five years old when her mother, father, two
aunts and an uncle left Quixeramobim's scorching
earth and set out for Fortaleza— winding up on the

coast in the unhealthy, crime permeated *bairro* (district) of Pirambú. The courageous priests and community activists (referred to as communist after the coup of '64) saved these sorry masses from the subhuman morass of urban servitude and utter destitution.

These organizer-agitators fired up dissolute migrants into a mighty fist capable of a knockout punch; the city fathers trembled as priests blessed the social organizers as doing God's ordained work. To educated reform minded Catholics, it was Liberation Theology, but to the opposition—the army and politicians of the ruling class whose greatest dread was Castro's Revolution spreading by radio and pamphlet to the tired, suffering masses of rural Brazil—to them, Liberation Theology was the cover for communist subversion.

The military coup of '64 saw many organizers forced to flee into hiding, or be jailed or worse. Even members of the Holy Church had to be very careful of the company they kept. Iraci saw Pirambú improve thanks to the local Padre and his mostly covert partnership with these social organizers. They cooperated in that common goal of improving living conditions for all of God's children, for the Glory of God and The Glory of "*Nosso* (our) *Brasil*". Together they had forced the city to build schools, to drill wells for clean water, to put in several health posts, to install electricity and lighting for the main street that ran some two miles through the *bairro*.

Of mixed success was the decree that essentially eliminated all bars and brothels from Pirambú. While the citizenry at large was happy with the ban, the ladies that plied their trade in establishments near their home dwellings, now had to either move across town to another less sanitized *zona* or commute. Eliminating prostitution involves much more than closing down the local brothels.

Destiny had it that I was hoping to see the Padre when I met Iraci. Blest was I with the good Padre's absence, and we went that night across town, to the area called *Farol,* where there was no Padre nor community spirited organizers to clean up the *bairro.*

Here life was rough and vital, tender yet cruel. *Farol* was where the docks were situated, where sailors from around the world roamed, where almost every structure was a bar or brothel, and where the ladies in "the life" lived.

Caixa Preta (Black Box) was our watering hole and urban retreat. Several of our Brazilian partying companeiras already lived in an abandoned bar which had been closed for over a year when the idea and opportunity came to us and our Brazilian host-nationals. *Farol* was one of the districts where the police left folks alone as long as a semblance of civility and a timely financial donation to justice were observed. We rented the *casa* for a nominal fee and set to work—the urban Peace Corps *safados* (sinners) and the ladies and Luis, our host national *companheiro* — younger brother to an officer of the law.

It was he who kept our supply of *maconha* (pakalolo) from exhausting, and it was our cooperative economics that stocked the bar for our evenings of entertainment. This made the ladies' situation less complicated in that they no longer had to traverse the streets and alleys of *Farol* in search of clients, but could dance and relax while traffic drifted in and out of the neighborhood.

We decided on the name and painted the interior totally black—*Caixa Preta*—a Black Box. Electricity was connected by a Peace Corps volunteer with a degree in electrical engineering. In a large spare room, behind the bar, we organized a school for the many loose youngsters that lived in *Farol* and had no school available to them. What could be more of a challenge for Peace Corps than to assist the most downtrodden of the impoverished? It proved to be a thin line between our desire to help and our own dissipation into wine, women, *maconha* (marijuana) and song which we had serendipitously fallen into.

Iraci and I got to Farol in the late afternoon, and as I had anticipated, her beauty was threatening to the other girls. Iraci was aloof, having worked with a wealthier clientele than the women of *Farol*. Introductions were icy with lots of *mal-olhado* (bad-eyeing), but because everyone was quite sober, there were no outbursts—not immediately.

I looked at our *companeiros* of *Farol* as a sampling in part of the hugely complex social stew that was and will forever be Brazil. Here, if you cared to you could be any color you wished, white, brown, black, yellow, red—green.

The hard life had left scars, both physical and psychological, on the women, as it must, invariably, on all persons who are forced, or rarely choose, to earn their daily bread by selling their charms. This base level of the economic struggle is a hard, cruel life and it shows—especially on those with years and miles of experience behind them.

Liquinha, with whom I was very close for several months, was a chestnut hued, hardy product of Maranhao State, situated just south of the mouth of the Amazon River. A desperately poor region where the air visibly hung above the wretched hovels that stretched around the city center of São Luis.

Liquinha was tough, and I was attracted to her hardy character which complimented her firm fullness of body—marred only by a nasty scar she bore as a result of a crude abortion undergone when she was sixteen. She was self conscious and quick in angered defense when anyone noticed or apologized for the mark, which in truth was hardly apparent, especially in low candle light.

Liquinha had the most rudimentary education— literate, but not practiced in her reading or writing. She was one of the several that helped teach the rudiments of literacy behind the *Caixa Preita*. And she was powerfully quick to evaluate situations and first to cross examine a hustler. Her heart of gold was all evident in her expressive bedroom eyes. Suffering had baptized her into that elite group of angels that would embarrass even Jesus, Son of God, with their empathy and concern for those innocents in need of a helping hand.

Was Liquinha a "Good Girl"? -absolutely! So how could she ply her trade daily amongst the variety of *"fregues"* (freight, customers or clientele) that paid her bills? Rum was Liquinha's fuel. It ushered her into the realm of self-abandonment, allowing the mask of eternal good times to dominate a basically shy, sensitive personality. With time and consistent indulgence, the shy and sensitive side are lost— inevitably and irretrievably—to the realities of prostitution. To rekindle that lost shy little girl within is most troublesome—opening the gates to heartache born of attachment. Attachment made inevitable when regular visits occur over a period of time with an attractive compatible "client". Yet that attachment to a "special friend" is what keeps many a young woman from disaster. It is the hope, the desperate dream of leaving "the life" and beginnng a real life of devotion, with a home and children.

Liquinha had only sparse hopes for such an escape; Iraci, on the other hand, was hell-bent on making her dream a reality—and she was neither naive nor weak-minded in how to get and keep her American Navy *namorado* and escape to paradise— to her Denver.

Fofo

Word of Fofo's death spread quickly and quietly. Muffled tones and contorted gasps spread throughout the room when India came in and whispered into Vera's ear. She whispered a message that, although inaudible, radiated among the group of women. Perhaps they were expecting bad news. In "the life" such news is not so surprising, but put into words, a common fear becomes a reality. All the ladies court the disaster of the botched abortion; this one had hit close to home.

The animosity brewing in the eyes of Iraci and Liquinha melted into a profound sense of camaraderie, much as a policeman or fireman feels the pain and loss of a fellow worker. The connection cannot be dismissed, even—no, especially, among those who share the burden of being the social underclass. No! The two women did not embrace and become born again sisters, but they did avert each others' eyes and shared in the overwhelmingly sad news of the young girl's death; yet Iraci knew the child not at all, and Liquinha only over the past several weeks. The initial silence built first to a low mumble and then to open exchanges of sorrow, sobs and inquiries as to the background and family of the poor dead girl. None of those gathered knew Fofo intimately, as she had been in Fortaleza only three months. The conversation drifted slowly to making funeral arrangements which seemed a relief from the weight of the "bad luck" event.

and there lay Fo-fo, calmer than we'd ever seen her.

The paved road gave way to ruts, rocks and the remnants of abandoned structures scattered amidst an untended field. In the far corner of a level area, near a few twisted trees, two workers with pick and shovel popped their heads above the hole they were digging. The mound of dirt suggested they must be finished with their chore as they climbed up out of the dark, sandy soil. The lead taxi pulled alongside the men and briefly exchanged words before moving thirty feet beyond to where some palm fronds covered the ground. Antonio, the driver of the lead taxi, got out of his car and indicated to the other cars and the jeeps where to park. There were now eight vehicles in the parade. The drivers disregarded Antonio's directions and cut their engines after finding a space to their liking; there remained generous space around the heap of earth, almost as if there was a fear of getting too close to the inevitable. The women slowly, solemnly made their way out of the vehicles and formed a wide arc around the mound of soil. The silence was broken by muffled cries as one of the girls ventured to the rim of the hole, peeked into the depths, and shuddering, jumped back to the security of the group of sisters. The group of prostitutes now numbered around thirty, perhaps twenty had joined in the caravan as our cars crossed town with our passengers tapping the horn and making quick stops to spread the word of the funeral for the unfortunate young girl lying in a box in the lead taxi. Several of the women knew each other, but many did not, yet they shared the common fate of "the life" and felt the common bond often celebrated together in the night life and now they were together to mourn. About the hole in the ground there lingered an uncomfortable silence. It lingered too long and perhaps would have led to the disintegration of the gathering had not Antonio stepped forward with reluctance at first, but soon his halting words gained strength and penetrated the hearts and minds of the congregation.

"Come my brother and sisters, let us put to rest Fofo Bautista do Vale. A young lady, branded whore by both the church and society's pillars, both, as is to be expected from their manner of thinking and judging, absent from our present, sad obligation." Antonio opened the back of his wagon-cab and slid the freshly painted wooden coffin partially off the tailgate where eager hands of the men and women secured it. The

box was open. Inside lay a light-skinned delicately
structured girl, hands folded above the waist atop a
simple white and pink cotton dress. Wild flowers were
scattered about the dead girl lending an air of
improbability to the scenario. One almost expected
young Fofo to rise with a joyous shout from the box,
toss the flowers to the wind, and locking arms with
her sisters, dance off into the dense forest just beyond
the burial site.

But Fofo did not jump out of her box, and no one danced into the woods. The gathered prostitutes were frightened as each saw in the dead girl their own body or that of the one to their left or right. It was the small print of the unwritten contract: a pregnant prostitute is a bankruptcy—a farmer with no crop; a fisherman with no line, no boat. Fofo tried to stay in business by having an abortion.

But something went wrong and this child of seventeen was dead in three days. She could have carried the baby to term, there were countless children of the street all over Brazil, but the decision to abort was fixed on a desire to "move up" in the "profession." Being young and into "the life" for only a year, she had been approached to join a group of women that worked wealthier clientele. She had to abort before the pregnancy began to show. The discussion among the girls was heated, for although the church had abandoned the girls, the Catholic upbringing was the fibre of the social morality, and to the women of this mind, abortion was worse than prostitution. Society and poverty had made these good girls whores, but the individual alone was responsible for the decision to abort. Fofo gambled and lost. Now she would be lowered into that foreboding dark hole. Was this her hell for all eternity? As the women looked on, each was struggling with the issue realizing—there but for the grace of God am I... As the coffin, carried by both men and women, was laid to rest atop the mound of dirt, objects, trinkets, and flowers were thrown to the dead girl. One tossed a necklace, another a photograph, a third some flowers; most wept openly now and a rhythmic contagion of shrieking began in earnest. Those who wept one moment were comforting another a moment later. Several went to the open wood box, peered in, made the sign of the cross, whispered some final words to the deceased, and weakly returned to the periphery, a picture of fear and despair. Antonio again stepped forward and asked the group if there was a person of a recognized church that would lead the group in a semblance of a ceremony. He knew there was none, but with three Peace Corps jeeps in the procession he asked anyway. His answer came in the form of silence. India, an Amazonian Indian with a slightly pocked face and large, gentle eyes, spoke loudly through an occasional deep sob. "Poor Fofo, she is just like us, we like her. She wanted to make more money to help her mother and brothers and sisters in Minas Gerais. She was so pretty and so young; now she is dead. It's sad; it isn't fair." One of the girls, too shy to step forward, sobbed, "Where is some church to say words over our dead sister? Didn't Jesus forgive sinners?" But her words had the effect of moving Antonio to step center and facing the group in the semi-circle he began: "The sins of this prostitute, for that is what she was, a *"puta,"* are nothing compared to the sins committed by those who refuse to witness the burial and the criminal neglect of the poor— thousands upon thousands of them—children with bulging bellies, adults aged 30, that thanks to malnutrition appear to be 60, and women —no—girls like this child in this box, barely more than a child, fallen—no, forced into "the life"; selling their flesh at an age when they should be full of a vigorous desire to study, to learn, to begin a family, a life for the Glory of Our Brazil and God above. But, no, our great and rich country has no mercy on the poor. Perhaps, God too is heartless. Forgive me this thought, but what are we to think when we are honest with ourselves, with this God that allows tender young women—girls—no more, no less than this Fofo—to be buried in this dark, deep hole. To die so young for the dead-end life of the streets. The rich are not smarter, nor more capable than this Fofo lying here. No! It is only because this little one, born poor, has had no opportunity to grow. She is like a delicate, tender flower about to blossom, when the cruel boot of oppression—the oppression of the poor by the rich, crushes the flower, crushes her as we witness our little sister here crushed, and now to be buried into this deep, dark earth. Who will remember this child thrown into the streets? Will the rich man who bought her body for a night remember her? Will the priest who refuses to acknowledge her passing? Will the God above receive her? If there is a God of Mercy and understanding, our Fofo will be received, received and held to the bosom of the Master who died for our Sins. For this God must surely see and know the failures and injustices of our world as it is today, not as it most certainly must be in Heaven. Let us bury this sister—and she is a sister as all women are our sisters and our mothers and our daughters. And let us remember her and say words to the Greater Authority that her delicate Soul will find in Eternity the Peace and Justice denied to her here on this earth."

Antonio had touched the heart of the matter. The gathering now had a positive glow—dare one say holy? The ambiguity of burying a lonely young prostitute a long way from home had taken on the more grand purpose because one man, a cab driver, who knew the workings intimately of the lives that surrounded him, had understood and made clear, profoundly clear, the reason for the suffering. He did not resolve the problem, no! but he made clear to everyone that being lowered into that dark hole was not only the young woman, but also part of all present - man and woman alike. And somehow, although he did not say it in words, all present knew that such suffering and waste was not God's will, but rather something sadly amiss here below in the Brazil they all loved.

The ride back through town was somber—a large wet blanket had been spread over the suffering. As an American, I felt some kind of remote guilt, knowing I could leave the arena of injustice and dead-end poverty my Brazilian companions were destined to live out to their end. But the sadness of the prostitutes in my jeep was different: it was based on empathy so personal that no words could reach down into those tortured souls and release the hurt. No words were spoken for most of the twenty minutes it took to arrive back at the *zona Farol*. A few sobs were choked back and tears were bottled and blotted with shared handkerchiefs, but it wasn't until the armada of taxi's, private cars and jeeps bounced over the hard packed sand and missing cobble stone street of the *zona* that the sparks of life began to spread among those who had caravanned across town to put Fofo to rest forever. To rest forever with her brief history of seventeen years of innocence, suffering, and the glimmer of a dream — an obscure and twisted, but brighter personal dream. But the tunnel of reality had collapsed–she would never emerge alive.

Upon arrival at the *Caixa Preita*, I slumped over the wheel while the passengers slipped out of the jeep and into the bar where flowers had been set on the tables and food was being prepared. I sat consumed in thought or maybe a secular prayer until I heard my name called from within. Making my way through the bar to the back room, I did not stop but went up the narrow, rickety stairs to the room above where Liquinha had spread out our large hammock. I fell into its waiting sway. Liquinha trailed in immediately behind, joined me with her tender caress, and together we openly wept and fell asleep.

When I awoke hours later, alone, the pulsating music from below was hell-bent on obliterating all traces of the morning's events. It was gathering dusk, the gang was into its cups, the rich aroma of *maconha* floated through the room and at the favorite corner table sat the family, strangers no longer: Americans born into plenty; Americans born into poverty and Brazilians born into a vibrant land of expectation and heart break. Liquinha's lip was curled, her eyes were glazed. She had been drinking.

A 'BLACK BOX' GATHERING

Asa de Barata

The letter came about a month later. We had almost forgotten about the project a week after having sent the ambitious inquiry off to the Stanford University Technical Assistance Program (SUTAP). It was during the interlude of a month that Jake "discovered" a new and exciting, reasonably priced hangout. I picked up the letter at the Peace Corps Office and bicycled across town, stopping only to appreciate the splendor of the setting sun and the timeless *jangadas (fishing rafts)* being hauled unto shore where the day's catch was examined and sold to restaurant buyers who were certain to haggle the price down to rock bottom, thereby guaranteeing the perpetual poverty of the fishermen. Their survival was day-to-day, and there seemed to be no way out of the cycle of misery, since the fishing co-op had collapsed the year before. And, like most everything else that went sour with the poor, it was part of God's Grand Design — *Si Deus quizer-* (if God wills it), which covered everything from a baby's death from dehydration to winning the national lottery; furthermore, one lived with *e Deus que paga* and - *e Deus que manda-* (God pays and God decides). God was supreme both above and below. It made life a lot simpler, but not easier. One of the local poet-singers had been silenced by the military dictatorship for his lyrics of resistance, one of which went: *Deus nao tem coracao* — God is Heartless.

Perhaps the letter I carried had some solutions to the problem we faced in trying to launch an industry right

in the *favela* — an industry that would put money into
the pockets of the ragged poor who were beaten down,
but refused to be counted out. Our little tightly knit
band of Peace Corps Volunteers and Brazilians lived
with and rooted for the underdog. We remained
faithful and supported our impoverished host
nationals, and perhaps, just perhaps, in this letter I
held in my hand from the technical assistance people
at Stanford University, there was the information that
would enable us to set up an industry in the *favela,*
perhaps to employ several of these downtrodden souls.
We had held several all night sessions in the bar,
investigated as best we could how to enter the market,
which from what we could gather, was dominated by
one supplier from Sao Paulo. What a score for Peace
Corps, if we, a handful of Americans thought to be
spending all our time carousing with Brazilian
woman, *maconha* and booze, managed to corner the
shellac market of Northeastern Brazil and perhaps
beyond. The idea had come to me one day while
working on a silkscreen printing project with a few
teen-agers and parents interested in health education.
In the States I had used shellac as a film for the
design on the "silk". In Brazil shellac is purchased in
flakes that look and feel a lot like cockroach wings —
hence the name *asas* (wings) *de barata* (of cockroach).
And hence my letter to Stanford's technical wizards,
asking them to unlock the secret of how to convert the
wings of this ubiquitous and indomitable pest that
sometimes looked and flapped around at night like a
small bat. By candlelight these *baratas* loomed

monstrous on the walls and several always managed to get through the mosquito net into the beds or hammocks in which we slept. Many a volunteer — usually a female, but not always — would freak out in the middle of the night because of a *barata* attack. This certainly contributed to a talented nurse, my wife, Suzanne's decision to call it quits, leave Brazil early and leave me with all those *baratas* and alluring Brazilian women.

I was a community developer; I had to live with and indulge in the lives of our host nationals. But now I had the chance to make a big score for American ingenuity — to convert the cockroach wings to shellac. But how? That is the question I put before our Stanford technocrats, and now, finally, I had the response. I would not open the letter until we all gathered that night at the *Caixa Prieta* (Black Box), our new little watering hole on the beach near the historic, rundown light house in the dock area of Fortaleza. Jake was just waking from the afternoon intervalo (siesta), his delicate little tiger of a woman, Gracinha, clinging to him in the king-sized hammock. Another PCV, Andy, was developing photos in an improvised dark room while India, his shapely, pock marked Amazonian lover, waited patiently for him to emerge into the fading light of day. It was always exciting to see the magic of photography-especially for the ladies, few of whom had schooling beyond the rudiments of functional literacy at best.

Several others from the neighboring houses and bars dropped by as was customary to survey our scene. Some of them had already been "working," and were half tanked on rum, beer, and cachaca. It was turning out to be a typical evening: we'd all drink, smoke *maconha* (marijuana), dance to the sounds of the Doors, Mamas and Papas, and the lively drag step *"fofo"* of the Nordestinos. Later, usually a few hours before sunrise, all would retire to their little rooms— a young man, a young woman, with their lust, their love, their dreams, their pains.

Such was the setting. But tonight would be different, for I had the letter that would unlock a secret that just might launch an industry that would lift the community by its bootstraps. Every volunteer harbored the dream of doing something significant for his host nationals. I was no exception, having in the past twelve months, working with the neighborhood Catholic Church started a hammock factory that functioned for awhile; launched a futile attempt to "invent" a cheap water filter for the poor with their plague of intestinal parasites; started the local kids with a program to gather donkey and oxen droppings for a methane gas conversion program (this idea had more than one local thinking I might be a bit "touched"); had moderate success in rigging a see-saw type clothes washer and numerous ventures in literacy and art co-operatives. But the shellac from cockroach wings—this I hoped would be a stroke of genius. Jake, Peter and some of the others were not so exuberant about the idea, but, — what the hell "this is Brazil" and anything might wake the "sleeping giant."

Around midnight, when everyone was half waxed, I decided to make my *pronunciamento,*—present, open, and read the letter we had for a month awaited. So here was Jake trying to explain to his Brazilian love how he happened to be born during a bombing raid in Nazi-occupied Latvia, to parents fleeing with the future of Latvia in their satchels and souls, and being carried across Europe in potato sacks, fleeing the insanity of the age. And of course he was telling it all in tortured Portuguese with the assistance of a pair of welder's-gloves-like hands and the animation of a determined Preguiça- (tree sloth), like the one I saw crossing a four lane street in downtown Manaus one day. "That must be a determined critter," I thought, "one whose territory had been physically divided by mankind's advance with his iron horse that needs a smooth path that divides the forest as a river divides the lay of the land." This path and the automotive traffic has been the death of many a traditional preguica whose fore-bearers had traversed that very space since Adam roamed naked in his own Amazon River paradise. But I drift.

The mood in the 'Box' was mellow. Luis, the local vice squad captain's younger brother, had garnered some choice smoke, and with the occasional outburst of hilarity, I savored the moment. It was a perfect night to surprise the gang with what to me had grown in my mind to be a sure thing— the keys to our future, for some of us would have stayed in Brazil were there a

steady flow of income — for Brazil was not a comfy
place if you are penniless. Our salary, meager as it
was, $75 a month U.S., was one helluva lot more than
our companions lived on. What more could one desire?
Jake, a Philosophy major from Rutgers, constantly
reminded us that Aristotle had declared man to be a
pleasure-seeking critter. Why contradict Aristotle? His
thoughts ruled Western civilization for over fifteen
hundred years. Even if one sees man and woman not
as pleasure-seeking but more as pain-avoiding, we
were there—warm weather, warm and friendly fun
loving people, splendid expanses of white sandy
beaches, electricity of sorts ("never turn your back on
an electric outlet", became a mantra) and we even had
a central domestic water tank with faucets and a sink,
a toilet and shower. Who could ask for more? We were
essentially without pain. And we were feeling no pain
that night I was about to read the notes by the
technocrats at prestigious Stanford University.
Technocrats of all dimensions; experts who advised
the community developers along the lines of how to
make those dreams of a better world come true
through science. And it was through science that I was
about to reveal the magic of the white man, whose
romance with investigative methodology was about to
secure for Peace Corps Brazil 17 the golden-brass ring
on the merry-go-round of American foreign policy.

I made the anticipated *pronunciamento* of the arrival
of the long awaited letter standing upon a stool,
looking down upon smiling faces caught in a moment
of heightened expectancy. I read:

Greetings Mr. Tomas Belsky and fellow Peace Corps
Volunteers of Brazil: Your intriguing letter dated, March 11,
1967 has generating much intellectual debate and research as
well as a good deal of humor here at SUTAP. Your aspiration to
form a shellac industry based on the wings of the much
maligned cockroach (*cu ca ra cha blattodea Brasilensis*) is not
unlike the noble quests of Don Quixote to garner rewards for
his romantic illusions concerning the fair maiden Dulcinea del
Taboso. Pure fantasy! And we at the laboratory are dismayed
that you — all of you college graduates — do not know that
shellac is produced from the wings of the tiny female "lac' bug
of India (Kerria laca, order Hemiptera, family Coccidae). There
is no way, despite the much touted wizardry of those chosen to
save the world via Peace Corps service, to make anything of
commercial value from cockroach wings. You might try feeding
said critters to chickens that quite conveniently convert the
damnable pest to protein in the form of delectable drum sticks.
We could send you a recipe for cooking a chicken, but we
believe at least one of you may already have a clue as to this
process. You might also try having neighborhood competitions
— cucaracha races— qualified contestants are placed alive,
dead center of a circle and released. The winner is the critter
first across the circumference, where it might be welcomed and
congratulated by a hungry hen. But, of course, some of the
lusty, boundless intellects receiving this note will surely
expand this idea and the direction we suggest for the
utilization of the bountiful natural resources with which you
and your American and Brazilian cohorts are inextricably
enmeshed.

If we at the University's Department of Technical Assistance
can be of further help, do not hesitate to contact us. In the
mean time, we here at SUTAP highly recommend that you stay
out of the noonday sun.

Reverentially yours,

Dr. N. Ernest Fumamais, Ph of D;
Dr. Phylis Snickermore, D of Ph.;
Dr. Arthur V. Schmeidlapp—research specialist

Well, we were appalled and taken aback, and a wee bit insulted by the overall tone of this response from a technical assistance team that is supposed to be totally supportive of us volunteers in the trenches at ground zero *Caixa Preita*. The laughs we garnered from this note are legendary. By the time we translated the letter into Portuguese for our host national fellow travelers to enjoy, numerous suggestions were tossed around that would adequately address their "altitude" and our indignation. After much soul searching it was decided to sacrifice a prime sample *barata,* whose wings we most carefully coated with three layers of shellac, placed into an artfully constructed coffin made from a match box, complete with external decor and a red velvet interior cushion for the comfort of the deceased. We took this package to the Peace Corps office from whence it went via the U.S. diplomatic pouch to the laboratory at Stanford University. We never heard from them again.

Introduction to Canindé

I was a Peace Corps volunteer in the Brazilian state of Ceará located in Northeastern Brazil. During my service there I experienced living in the interior of the state for one year and then was transferred to the capital city, Fortaleza. From this experience I was able to understand the difficulty the thousands and thousands of peasants were made to endure in their move to the capital seeking an easier life away from the drought plagued interior (sertão).

The trip from the busy, colorful capital, Fortaleza, into the interior is an experience not only in distance, but also in time—perhaps a hundred years, at least, into the past when electricity, plumbing, paved roads and other amenities of modern living are considered marvels, which indeed they are. The pilgrims heading for the miracle city of Caninde travel by truck, horse, oxcart, jeep and by foot; common to all is the baggage and animals—chickens, pigs, and goats are interwoven in a network of sprawling life with squawks, bleats, grunts and cries of pain and cries of joy, laughter and song. It is an unforgettable sight. Nothing had changed for scores of years until the past three decades, perhaps my experience was the tail-end of an ancient ritual and tradition.

While the interior of the entire Northeast is a stronghold of large landholdings and extreme social divisions reminiscent of medieval Europe, the inhabitants are nothing if not tough and resilient with an almost inexplicable attachment to a land that is harsh and severe—except when the rains come. When there is abundant rainfall, cattle are fat and crops are thick in the fields, like lovers on the mend, all is forgiven; workers toil from sun up to sundown for a wage barely able to sustain the numerous children that overflow their mud and stick houses. The Catholic Church is the dominant social institution and literacy is at best privileged upon fifty percent of the population. Poets sing the news from town to town and are an esteemed class, carefully observed and respected by the masses of landless peasants and their lords and masters (latifundiários), as well as the Church hierarchy.

Canindé

It hadn't rained for two years and the earth was parched, cracked and whirled about in bursts of wind that swept through the valleys amongst the rolling hills. Although there was no close-knit procession of vehicles, we knew we were part of something much larger. The hundred miles from Fortaleza to Canindé were dotted with groups heading for the very same destination—a church dominated community, all but forgotten save for the religious festival that drew thousands of visitors, would be saints and hopeful repentant sinners, young and old alike, of good health and poor.

Between those wounded through the harsh, unforgiving environment were the crippled—those with twisted and missing limbs, with impaired sight, speech and/or hearing. Our Peace Corps jeep passed them on the dusty road. At first there were sparse groups on horseback, on mules, in carts drawn by oxen and babies in carts drawn by goats. As we left the capital, the main road turned to dirt and received the traffic from smaller roads—trails, really, that led to the settlements of several houses sometimes frighteningly far from any trace of modern civilization. For all events and purposes these tiny communities were devoid of all the benefits and headaches that accompany electricity, piped-in water, schools and health facilities. They were actually caught in a life rooted in the nineteenth century at the very latest. And much of what appeared on the road to Canindé was rooted back hundreds of years across the Atlantic Ocean and the tired, worn pages of Church history, in the old world of Portugal and its imperial legacy of colonized native Americans, and African slave labor. An occasional pair of blue eyes and blonde hair on dark skin attest to the half century when Holland dominated these same lands.

Lives are founded upon the rock of the Will—the Will of man or the Will of God. Modern civilizations have nudged God aside, for better or for worse, and assumed responsibility for what transpires to a greater degree than ever before in human history. But not these pilgrims on the road to Caninde this hot Friday morning. The first one I saw caught me by surprise. I was expecting to see peasants in tattered clothes, carrying malnourished infants, and *caboclos* (hillbilly types), shoeless, leading a mule loaded down with the few essentials these subsistence survivors could gather together for the trip to Caninde, but the sight of a man ambulating on his knees in the lead of a group of a dozen or so followers, stunned me. And I turned to my friend, Mauricio, for an explanation. "There will be many of these," he said, noticing my puzzled look. He started to smile almost cynically, but was cut short by Antonio, his bosom buddy (and chicken-fighting partner), who nudged me from his seat in the rear of the jeep. "He made a *promessa*—a plea to God for help, for mercy, a trade in kind. He promised to walk the distance—hundreds of miles even—to Caninde on his knees, if God would grant such and such favor—could be the spared life of a child, or the avoidance of a dreamt up catastrophe. Some do the walk—and suffer quite a bit— then, they anticipate the reciprocal benevolence from on High; others receive God's end of the bargain first, and then make the journey on their knees."

"Will they make it? This is a fifteenth century mindset," I thought, observing the group of pilgrims as we passed. It would take them forever to cover the hundred miles at the snail's pace set by the penitent in front. On his knees he moved forward over the dusty, parched earth; there were no pads for his tortured knees, arms were raised in longing exaltations, moans and lamentations were uttered from his lips, and the chorus was picked up and repeated by those following. The thumping of fists on chests kept time to a jingle of bells on a goat's neck. The whole affair crawled along across the parched earth and relentless sun.

"They'll never get there before the end of the Festival", I thought out loud.

"God will intercede for most of them," Antonio allowed. "Only the most possessed will walk all the way on their knees. A truck will stop and offer a ride—most will take it. A priest will see their plight and acting in God's name, allow them to ride if opportunity arises. *Se Deus Quiser*— if God Wills it." The *sertao* runs on God's will in the lives of these peasants. God had denied the peasants their rainy season and they knew it was because of their failure as followers of Jesus, the Church and the priest. A trip to Caninde, and taking confession in one of the dozens of curtained confessionals on the central square and around the church, could atone for the non-specific offense in the eyes of God.

It was a kind of give and take, a balance of power in the affairs of Heaven and Earth. Most of the inhabitants of the *sertao* paid some respect to the formula; others, usually those with the weapons and tools of literacy, sought at least in part, a rational explanation for the suffering in the secular realm. If it was not God, then it certainly had to be the government somewhere down south. The road wound and wove up and down the rolling hills of the drought stricken earth. From the high points one could see in all directions and what one saw was the same: lines of pilgrims moving in steady streams into the main road to Caninde. There were more vehicles as we grew closer to our goal. Trucks were overflowing with passengers clinging to improvised handgrips. Baggage and animals—chickens, pigs, and goats in a great cacophonous symphony of the life of the underclass. Squawks, bleats, grunts and laughter, songs and exaltations emanated from these flat bed trucks that carried the freight and passengers of the lower classes all over Northeastern Brazil. Parrots' perch—*Pau de Arara* they call these transport vehicles for their packed condition, like parrots on a branch with literally no space unoccupied—none.

So important is the Festival at Caninde to the *sertanejos* that *Pau de Araras* were arriving from all directions. From as far south as northern Bahia they came, from Pernambuco to the east and Paraiba, and Alagoas. But mostly they came from Ceará. It seemed the whole of the *sertao* was emptying into Caninde for several days of religious and earthly revelry. Believers and nonbelievers alike—they all came. Penitents, priests, and poets; hustlers, merchants, priests, and prostitutes. Some for heavenly, some for earthly gain; they all packed into the town center filling it with a vibrant, throbbing *Joie de Vivre*—celebrating the

promise, the reward, the poetry, and the music. Again
the secular and the celestial divided the town. Priests
set up confessionals at every possible space within two
blocks of the church. And every confessional had a
waiting line that extended around a corner where it
merged with another waiting line of sinners. The
mood in these gatherings would shift from solemn to
exalted as the burden was lifted from an agonized
soul.

Amongst these lines about the confessionals walked
scores of children, adults and mendicants, pleading,
cajoling, exhorting persons to indulge them a moment
(*pelo amor de Deus*) for the Love of God—to purchase
this icon of Sao Joao (St. John) or that trinket of Padre
Cicero— the rebellious local priest hero of the poor in
the 1920's who marched on the capitol. The flurry of
activity that surrounded the Church was somehow
carnival-esque—but not rowdy or rude, for the
grounds of the Church were held sacred. In the very
front of the Church at town center there gathered a
seemingly endless procession of incapacitated persons.
These penitents had fashioned from various
inexpensive materials, usually wood, string and paint,
replicas of their sought after cures. A man without
movement in an arm, made of a carved tree limb a doll
with the afflicted limb rigidly fixed, while the other
appendages, fashioned with dowel or nail, would
swing freely. Here was a growing pile of spiritually
inspired craft. There were paintings, carvings in the
round, relief sculptures, roughly hewn logs resembling
legs, arms, heads with various afflictions indicated.

The items grew in number before my eyes. From a few the first day to numerous and then countless by the third day. On the last day the stack was a full twenty five feet high and thirty feet across. Snatches of this have remained vivid in my mind over these past forty-five years. Here

was an isolated incidence of ritual that survived from the Age of Faith into the Age of Reason and beyond into our Age of Science. The icon, the Faith, the purification of the afflicted and the miracle—the cure. Did it work? Does it work?

I recall one evening standing in the multitude around the great heap of manikins and items in the front of the Church. There were many priests around and numerous collection baskets overflowing with very worn and often undecipherable crumpled *cruzeiro* notes. Amidst the splashing of holy water and pleas for mercy, a man in tattered clothes on crutches ushered forth, shouting for all there gathered to hear his fervent appeal to God for mercy and relief from his suffering. This man, all eyes focused on him, hurled his crutches onto the heap where countless other crutches protruded, and walked off. No, he danced off to the shouting and breast-beating hallelujahs that ensued. *"Milagre! milagre!"* miracle! was heard throughout the stirred hundreds. Within the minute, another man, better dressed in store bought clothes and relatively neatly groomed, shouting hosannas, sprang forth and cast his crutches too, into the pile. Seconds later he took one shaky step forward, staggered and crumbled over. Down he went, down to the dusty blood red earth of the Church grounds amidst groans and lamentations from the multitude. Agonized and bewildered, he rose with the help of his friends, one of whom retrieved his crutches from the pile. Together amidst shouts of disappointment and consternation they dissolved into the confusion of the throng.

To believe or not to believe. I made my way through the animated groups of pilgrims, away from the church, wandering as the mind wonders when presented with options. I found myself in a place where voices were punctuated with laughter and the sound of the hollow-twang of *Nordestino* guitars permeating the thick darkness.

Drifting toward the sounds of merriment that my soul yearned for, I spied an old man in tattered rags, a tired straw hat half covering his scraggy, bearded, unwashed face, seated against a faded scarred wall. A handful of persons was gathered about as the wrinkled figure fiddled on a home-made two stringed instrument. The sound that emanated was eerily seductive, seeming to convey the isolation and endless suffering of the *Nordestino*. I joined with the few around the performer and quickly became aware that he was blind and had traveled to Ceará, God knows how or from where, certainly with hopes, dreams, and prayers of the Miracle. Over and over he coaxed the same refrain from the instrument tucked somewhere beneath his rough beard. "What suffering," I thought, "how much can these desperate innocent children of God endure?"I peeled off a 500 *cruzeiro* note and dropped it into his clay bowel and re-entered the stream of buzzing humanity toward what appeared to be general merriment.

The tavern was open to the dusty cobbled street on two sides. Electric lights, powered by a generator somewhere, yielded only enough illumination to produce dense, large shadows on the rough-hewn tables and straw-littered concrete floor. Patches of straw seemed to appear, not for effect, but for the necessity of feeding goats, horses and oxen that were everywhere in Caninde for the much heralded activities.

While the church tends to the soul of the faithful, the *Repentistas* tell of God's mysterious ways that often are recognized through the follies of mankind. In areas where illiteracy runs sometimes as high as eighty percent of the people, the poet is an important indicator of the ways of the world. Quick to glorify God in heaven, the *Repentista* does not shrink from emphasizing the human (sometimes too human) aspect of His representatives down here on earth. Into the exotic and harsh life of the *sertanejo*, these singing poets bring the mirror reflecting and projecting the familiar struggles and ironic joys of life, where even the death of an infant brings bitter joy to parents and siblings who will not have to further divide the little food available.

Often they tell tales in harsh humor, satire, and total absurdities; they sing of a woman who through pagan ritual turns her husband into a goat, or the story behind *Lampiao* (a Billy the Kid type folk hero), and the good Padre Cicero—a spiritual—activist priest in the vein of Martin Luther King Jr., who marched across the State of Ceará with a rag tag retinue of true believers.

The folk tradition is alive and well this night in Caninde. The *cachaça* (cane whiskey) is flowing, the beer is abundant and the poets in voice. I found a chair at a table with folks who immediately welcomed me and someone placed a bottle of Brahma Chope—a fine beer in any country—in front of me. "A sanctuary," I thought, "sanity and calm in the middle of the fervor."

Mauricio and Antonio had seen me on the street and somehow drawn me, as with a magnet, to find a seat across the room from them. They were responsible for the beer. By the time I had taken my first swallow a woman was at my side eyeing me as only a woman in "the life" can. Before I could muster an excuse for not joining her, Mauricio and Antonio were at my side between the woman and me. They realized the potential danger to a foreigner who refuses an offer from an inebriated prostitute on one hand; and on the other hand, should he accept the offer, danger from a drunk or sober nationalist who sees his physical intervention as an advance for Brazilian sovereignty, or even moral heroism in the face of his perception of the wave of foreigners in his country deflowering chaste maidens. A refrain I heard many times. Ludicrous as the situation seemed, I was more than glad to be rescued and seated with persons familiar with all eventualities in this raw backland. Mauricio and Antonio had an impressive roll of fresh *cruzeiros* newly won from the afternoon chicken fights held in a quaint ring directly across town from the church. Both these honest, hard-working men, seldom, if ever, had money enough to buy beer in town, much less to buy one for an *Americano*, all of whom were considered to have an endless supply of *cruzeiros* waiting to be tapped.

Antonio talked to the woman, capturing her attention, and Mauricio pointed to the stage where two *violeiros* were adjusting their seats and guitar strings. But before the musical exchange began, a disturbance directly outside spilled over the doorway and into the tavern directly amongst us patrons. Several persons were physically trying to dissuade a man on crutches from joining the patrons of the tavern. The pulling, shoving and resisting was loud and physical. An opening in the bedlam allowed me to recognize the man on crutches as the better-dressed individual whose attempt to receive the cure of faith had failed.

From the verbal outbursts it was apparent that this man, perhaps forty years of age, was turning over a new leaf—a return to the old ways of wine, women and song. He was determined and convinced of his decision; his attendants, but one, were trying to dissuade him. This one, showed himself to be of the leader's persuasion. He cleared a way into the tavern through the crowded street, led the group in through the open side of the tavern and readied a chair for his friend, boss, and colonel—the center of attraction, to relax in. He did this all without uttering a word. And he succeeded, for apparently, those who wanted to pass the frolicking tavern had conceded to his and the master's demands to make a short rest stop inside this conveniently located house of entertainment. The pulling and grappling wound down as *Seu Augusto*, that's what they called him, was released from the feverish concerns of the four who had been pulling and cajoling for the entire two blocks from the church. With a groan of relief he settled into the readied chair.

The poets, arranged ground level and tavern central in positions half facing each other, slammed into their instruments releasing the unique and indescribably haunting refrain. This is the medium of melody that carries the verses revealing the history and culture of the people of the *sertao*. The verses are absurd, humorous, fantastic and ingenious—not to say spontaneous. Before they got through the first verses of introduction *Seu Augusto* interrupted everything to thank God for his liberation:

Da licenca aqui, gente boa
So quero dizer este testimonio
Gracias ao Deus Poderoso
Que vive no Ceu,
Sou livre destes diabos das Igrejas
Agora nao vou falar nisso, nao
Vou gostar da musica, poesia, e sabedoria
Destas artistas que nos honoram
Com sua presenca em nossa capital metropolitana
O Caninde do Ceará em Nosso Brasil
Obrigado por sua amable atencao.

[Good people,
may I have your attention!!

I want to thank Almighty God in Heaven
that I am free from those devils in the church
No more of this, now
I am going to enjoy the music, poetry and wisdom
Of the artists who this evening honor us
with their presence in our
metropolitan capital
Caninde of Ceará in our Brazil.
Thank you for listening to me.]

Seu Augusto's speech calmed the last of the entourage that had tried to dissuade him from entering the tavern. Everyone's attention focused again on the man and woman *Repentistas* who nodded their approval of Augusto's blessing. The tavern had filled with patrons and the curious; they were crowded in several deep in the sides open to the street. The line between the sidewalk and the tavern interior was totally obscured. Word had spread that among the numerous poets were two of the most acclaimed *Repentistas* of the region. And they were matching up, both having been drawn to Caninde for the wildly popular festivities. The air was tense and dynamic with anticipation. It was a family, community event with good times for all parties. The overlay of religious destiny held much sway over the region that this night's poetic match-up was believed to be arranged by the Almighty Himself—and the poets would act accordingly—as they always did.

Now the twanging rhythms receded and two
repentistas a man and a woman (a rare spectacle in
itself) nodded to each other in a gesture of mutual
respect and the lady poet threw back her head, sent
her raven black hair flying under her leather *chapeu*
and let loose a strong, deep-voiced, clear refrain.
Suddenly the tavern fell under her spell and silence
punctuated her verses:

Good evening everybody
Tell me, how do you do?
My name is Ana Roxina
and I've come to play for you
I'm a poet and a woman
Some say this cannot be
but I'm a child of these backlands
and spon tan e i ty.

She made the tavern resound with her ferocious
strumming of the strings, looked over to Severino who
picked up the rhythm and with a voice as raw as the
parched earth began:

Hola and welcome sertanejos
and visitors from afar
I'm Severino Simeao
known as the Shooting Star
for my style's quick as lightning
and my verses give a jolt
versifiers who stumble
will be measured with my rope.

Again they dueled on the guitar several rounds and
Ana Roxinha belted forth:

Severino is a devil
he's a serpent and a scam
Hides behind his mama's skirt
and calls himself a man.
I will grab his smelly mustache
twirl his tongue beneath this thumb
Confuse his mind

confound his verses
Chase him back from whence he comes.

Severino looked a bit uneasy at the force of his female opponent's approach, but he nodded his head in approval as he drove the devil of the backlands out of his guitar and led into his retort:

Such a pretty face to look at
and such harsh, cruel words I hear
Shall I return the compliment and drag her by the hair?
Ahhh, No! Severino is a gentleman
By my mother's prayer I am
But this tigress needs a lesson
And God knows that I'm the man
Who can tie her tongue with verses
Soap her mouth to end the curses
Turn her over on this knee
Till she begs a kiss from me.

The men in the audience roared their approval of Severino's audacious response. Between verses exchanged the tavern erupted into applause, shouts, laughter and congratulations to the most recent singer's slam. When the acclaim receded into an animated murmur, the guitarist's refrain, too, diminished allowing for the opponent's response. Severino and Ana Roxinha were entering into a brutal exchange of insults and personal heroics, and the audience loved it; this was *Repentista Nordestino* at it best. I too was swept into the festivities: The *cachaca* was flowing—I had one, then another amidst shouts and a bit of hearty back slamming. I unrolled some of my bright red-orange *cruzeiro* notes, placed them on the table to the approval of the entertainers, and saw those crisp notes transported, unceremoniously, into the leather hat upside down on the littered table in front of the dueling poets. The atmosphere was electric and the generator of the magic was the hollowed out mysterious deep throated twang of the guitars and the voices that carried the challenge between the poet combatants.

I was becoming drunk on *cachaça* and the atmosphere, but to leave the scene was unthinkable. Everyone within listening distance of the duet was drawn into the fray, anticipating the next round of bragging and insults flung upon their adversary. I remembered for a moment the scene in front of the Church only hours before—severe, somber, dark and tragedy-laden. Here, a hundred yards away, was ribald merriment. I stole a glimpse at Seu Augusto now surrounded with women and well-wishers. He seemed in his element, and his retinue that so recently had tried to drag him away from the tavern was now adjusted to the noisy atmosphere. Perhaps they too were indulging, but my senses were blurred to the particulars on this point; clearly though, none of them had left the scene, although, most had settled to the rear of the little man who so recently had been denied the miracle and was now thoroughly enjoying the secular joys of the tavern. My head was beginning to spin when Ana Roxinha's voice broke through the haze:

Beg a kiss from this sad poet?
already dead but doesn't know it—
Best he bow his face in shame
leave this place while still he can
Mind of monkey, face of goat
broken verses, rasp in throat
Homeless, loveless, soft of bone
Gone! Be gone to Satan's throne.

Here the women of the tavern let loose a shrill cacophony of applause, whistles and cat calls, overwhelming the laughter and merry growls of most of the men who seemed content to let Roxinha and her supporters rule the moment. But when several well lubricated ruffians rose in vulgar verbal tirades in support of Severino, encouraging him to give the *coup de grace* to the smiling *poeta*, the tavern proprietor took center floor and insisted the singers shift their direction away from personal attacks and into a rhyming format that demanded spontaneity and poetic prowess called *oito em quadrao* or eight rhyming verses. The patrons were divided in their response to this demand, and for a moment it seemed that the crowd would get unruly.

Mauricio leaned over to me and shouted in my ear that things could become nasty. I remembered a time he told of in Fortaleza when a couple of *repentistas* went beyond a certain line of respect and began insulting families of their opponents. The result was a riot in which two people were shot dead and several others knifed. Antonio, the quieter of the friends, who even wore a necktie in town from time to time, was quick to second the motion that we leave. My mild and somewhat inebriated protests were disregarded and in a few moments we were on the outside leaving the fomenting crowd clamoring for more action.

Outside the stars had filled the sky and the dry chill of *sertao* nights was setting in. The streets were spotted with peasants in their flour-sack, home stitched clothing. There were shouts and cries of children, of agony and of love to be heard amidst the crowing of roosters and the grunts, groans and snorts of invisible livestock. The clear night silhouetted houses that lined the dusty street leading to our *pensao*—rooming house. The sturdy little lady that ran the operation was at the door with a fixed, stern, quizzical expression on her wrinkled face. She looked like she wanted to scold us for reasons known only to herself, the sertanejos, and the Church, but only crossed herself several times beat her breast with a closed fist and bade us enter. Mauricio gave her a wink as we stumbled past into the darkened corner where three *redes*—hammocks—we had mounted earlier awaited our immediate collapse.

Brazilian Mojo

Iraci II

Iraci asked me to help her get to America. Her American navy lover supplied her with plenty of money for the paper work and she was willing to spend it for the escape out of "the Life." My role was to help her navigate through the paperwork at the embassy in Recife, Pernambuco, some thousand miles south of Fortaleza. She figured that as an Americano I would know who to slip money to to make things happen. I would travel by bus and stop in Recife on my way to Rio for the flight back to USA. I had a Peace Corps friend who, like myself, worked with a Liberation Theology priest in a favela of Recife and I thought an exchange of notes might be interesting. Iraci returned to Recife with my promise to help her in three weeks or so when I terminated. Those three weeks proved to be an extended bacchanal. A couple of our host national lady friends were being rotated to Recife and offered us comfort should we visit them. It so happened that Jake and I worked out a schedule for such a visit. I was reminded of the trip to Recife and the obstacles before getting to see the ladies, thirty years later in Hawai'i as I sat waiting for my turn at the dentists office. I kept a running narrative of my ventures in Brazil in a series of notebooks that were lost through the stupidity of the owners of a storage firm in Hilo (AA storage—avoid them!) and my own situation of financial distress. They saved the wood file cabinet, but sent to the dump my notes of Brazil, Nicaragua and Hawai'i. The following is a recollection of that trip to the Hotel California in Recife

December 4, 2006 Written while waiting for the dentist in Kea'au, Hawai'i.

Toothache

Nothing like a toothache to remind one constantly that we have teeth. It's been a long time, maybe fifteen years, since I last saw a dentist—John Leonard—may he be blest with the presence of Jesus (he was a Catholic Independent). John did re-filling of fillings that the gold (Peace Corps Brazil gold) fell out of. It's an intriguing tale of how a renegade Jersey boy got a few solid gold fillings in Rio de Janeiro back in 1967. I guess I could start the pertinent segments of the story in the colorful city of Fortaleza, some 1500 miles on the coast, north of Rio. Some of the girls at the Caixa Preita (Black Box) nightclub suggested that Jake and I visit them when they transferred to Recife, down the coast several hundred miles. It happened that their rotation coincided with my termination date in Rio, so a stop over in Recife would be a bonus before returning to the States and the turmoil that every young person anticipated at that time. Jake, another volunteer, was in love with several ladies that would meet us at the Hotel California in Recife.

On the bus south Jake stayed mostly drunk, which complicated a typically chaotic bus ride in Northeastern Brazil—late, hurried and harrowing, punctuated by flat tires and horrendous rain and mud stops which necessitated passengers sinking above the ankles in the red earth to push the growling monster Mercedes Benz free of the thick, slick muck that sucked us all down and in like a hungry greedy lover anxious that she not be abandoned. These unexpected stops are a story in themselves, but that is left for another time.

We made it to Recife several hours late, in the early evening, and made our way to the Hotel California on the coast, overlooking a white sandy beach. The hotel proved to be a condo type affair some thirteen stories high, each of which had a madam that oversaw the numerous young Brazilian prostitutes who carried on in a relatively orderly fashion. One madam for each floor of the edifice. The Madam's role is to filter the clientele and direct them to services.

Our friends were on the eleventh floor. Our madam was a large German woman, Hazel, who spoke good English and poor Portuguese, although she had lived in Brazil longer than in the U.S. She looked us over in our tired, dirty aspect and after some delicate explaining, she ushered us into her apartment where she extended us a gracious hospitality which included a shower, a change of clothes, and roast chicken dinner with drinks and *maconha*, the Brazilian version of pakalolo or marijuana. It was wonderful getting cleaned up after the bus adventure. The clothes were misfits, but clean and much appreciated. Refreshed, we settled down to enjoy a generous roast chicken dinner.

Whenever we asked about our lady friend, Iraci, Hazel deflected us with—"*depois, mais tarde*," later. We ate heartilly and enjoyed the fine Brazilian beer Chope. Jake and I managed to slip onto the balcony to smoke some choice *maconha* and we were feeling quite ecstatic as we prepared to depart good Hazel's company for that of the ladies we had come to visit.

To our surprise, Hazel had locked the door and stood in the doorway of her bedroom adorned in a flimsy pair of delicately embroidered pink panties. She ushered us into her large bedroom and we soon realized it would be to no avail to try anything other than to comply with this generous hostess' desires. Besides, as I always reminded others, it would be a violation of Peace Corps ethics and purpose to show a lack of courtesy to a host national, especially one that had treated us so nobly. Hazel sat on the edge of her king-sized bed, dressed in exquisite pink panties only.

She was a largish woman in her mid forties, blonde and graying, buximous on top with short stump-like legs that exuded an aura of enormous strength. Her presence was disarming and Jake and I immediately realized we had been drafted into her services. We had to perform before we would be released to the ladies awaiting us. It wasn't such a bad deal, Hazel had been very kind to us and now she had her own needs.

I took the first shift while Jake rolled another macro joint. I soon found that we had underestimated Good Hazel's passions. She was close to twice my weight and writhed about like a whale in shallow waters; after being tossed about somewhat mercilessly, I called out and reached for Jake as tag team wrestlers do. He crawled into the fray and being better endowed, *shlanger*-wise, calmed and soothed madam Hazel momentarily.

It was during this respite that I made my way back into the kitchen and over-zealously chomped down on one of the remaining chicken drumsticks, and while contemplating our fate, realized that I had broken off a large portion of a lower molar. This unsettled me, but did not relieve me of the task at hand, and Jake was now calling for help from the bedroom.

Jake, who was built like a fullback, was locked in a scissor grip of Hazel's oaktree-like stumps. I rejoined the struggle, but the good madam would not release my exhausted comrade. Every time I lifted one of the heavy limbs a moan of protest bellowed forth from our hostess. Gathering our wits and working in unison Jake and I at last managed to soothe sweet Hazel and shortly thereafter, having met all the requirements, were released to visit Iraci and her network of cohorts.

My broken tooth would be tended to days later when I got to Rio de Janeiro, where a delightful young American-trained *bossa nova*-strumming guitarist/dentist put the gold in the broken tooth. While we waited for something or other in my mouth to set, he played the guitar and told me of the many advantages of remaining in Brazil. He said I was a *Carioca do coracao* — a native of Rio at heart. This is quite a compliment as *Cariocas* are noted for their robust passions and lively sense of humor. But I had domestic squabbles to tend to in *Gringolandia*.

A few days later I found myself in a frazzled *America do Norte*, unsure of myself and my place in the universe. But I would frequently roll my tongue over the large gold filling in my jaw and memories of other climes and rhymes never failed to come to mind.

But before I got to Rio I had one more adventure with Iraci, an episode that shook me into the reality of how dangerous an impetuous, one dimensional individual—especially a beautiful woman—can be.

Irací III

Early the next morning, Iraci was racing about her apartment more frantic than reasonable. In a strong insistent voice she got me out of bed, and like a martinet, cleared the couples from her rooms, explaining this was the day her amigo, Tomas, would take her to the American Consulate office to get the papers necessary for her trip to America. This was a woman with a plan deeply ingrained in her identity.

She was stunningly beautiful above all, but also possessed a quick intelligence and a domineering personality. It was easy to understand how a young American in the US Navy would be proud to have an Iraci on his arm when he returned home to Denver. His parents, on the other hand, might be of another mind.

Iraci's greatest asset was a physical beauty blended from the historical mix of peoples from Portugal, Africa and the natives of South America. Perhaps she knew her beauty would fade with time, leaving a literate but uneducated woman of "the life." This, she calculated, was her one chance to grasp what many considered a fantastical dream, and she was focused on not letting it slip away through her lack of focus on her goal.

Not that Iraci was above the other woman in carrying on at parties. She was a queen-pin—a natural leader. Her apartment was the biggest and most comfortably furnished. The other ladies always brought their patrons to her room to show them they were high class. They were prostitutes-yes, but they were high class—even elegant. It was all about money, and Iraci had a dresser drawer full of pink ten thousand *cruzeiro* notes with the elegant face of Santos Dumont peering out from under a stylish French *chapeu.*

Santos Dumont is, to Brazilians, really the first person to fly an "airplane." An honor the North Americans had wrestled from them and bestowed upon the Wright Brother. Iraci, of course, knew nothing of this, but she knew that her Navy *"namorado"* could keep her well supplied with these liberating pink notes. But his tour of duty was ending and he would soon return to *America do Norte* and she was determined to be at his side when the big jet plane touched down in Denver, or Miami or Los Angeles.

She was hungry for a new life and I, an Americano with far less money than she, had what she needed— the know how to facilitate her exit from Brazil: the understanding and facility with English and the language of the bureaucracy.

With these thoughts racing through my mind I marveled at how this woman could be so completely different from last night's Iraci — carefree, flamboyant, extravagant—perhaps neurotically over indulgent in an enthusiastic bacchanal — smoking , drinking, pill popping — singing and earning her the odd nick-name: *Urubu*—the huge red-necked, ugly buzzard that hovers so majestically above cities all over Brazil—effortlessly navigating the most delicate air currents. Iraci earned her moniker, *Urubu,* because she is said to have, under numerous intoxicants, desired to fly like the great buzzard from her eleventh story balcony. She was, after all, a young confused woman, prone to all the misfortunes that befall those in the shackles of poverty and deprivation. Now she saw a way out—with a man of means that loved her, and would call her wife, and take her to his home in far away Denver.

By eight o'clock we were in a cab heading for the American Consulate in downtown Recife. For the early hour, I was surprised to see the number of people crowding into the American Consulate. The elevator had a long line that extended and twisted into a soft "S" across the entire foyer. Iraci's energy seemed to increase as we exited the taxi. She grasped my hand and almost dragged me through the crowded entrance with the busy patrons of official US-Brazilian business.

All the while she was speaking softly, then loudly and not overly coherent: With the papers she sought in hand it would be easy for her and her man to leave Brazil together. So obsessed was she with her ambition, that perhaps she did not realize her crude behavior, which I, foolishly, failed to check earlier that morning. Iraci in her personal rapture, broke into the elevator line close to the door in front of a long line of patient individuals, and I, like a damn fool, allowed myself to be dragged behind her.

Numerous persons were miffed by this rudeness and some mumbling was observed; Iraci was oblivious to all around her. When the elevator door opened we were part of the dozen souls squeezed aboard for the lift upward. As the elevator began its jerky rise, a thin, small mesomorph of a Brazilian gentleman in a white suit with a pencil thin mustache and an angry angle to his brows, pushed his way directly in from of me. "*Coronel,*" I thought, "a pissed-off *coronel, Lord and Demon of the backlands.*"

His sweet smelling cologne was liberally sprinkled upon crisp white pants, spotless white jacket, and glistening boots—the uniform of the *colonel*—(Cor.o.nel) feudal lord of the lawless backlands— the *Sertao* (rhymes with noun) interior of Northeastern Brazil. Peasants of the *Sertao* were not free citizens, but property of this or that *coronel*. This particular *coronel* was less than pleased by our having cut into the elevator line, and as a gentleman and upstanding lord of *machismo*, his anger was not, could not, be leveled upon the still chattering Iraci, but on me, the poorly dressed white *Americano* being dragged about by a Brazilian hussy, who had violated his space, honor and sense of decorum.

He fixed his little coffee colored eyes into mine and reached into his crisp white jacket and pulled out a small revolver, which he proceeded to press into my chest, and, before God and the compressed members of the captured audience, enunciated a phrase that has stuck to me over these many years: "*A brincadeira e com outra!*" which may be rendered in English— "No one pulls that shit on me!" Or "No one fucks with me as you have so done!" or "who the hell do you think you are!"

Well I sobered right up with the pistol pressed to my chest. Iraci proved to me how stupid she could be in that instant; she let out a barrage of insults to this viscous little *coronel* who absorbed her insults by pressing the little nuzzle of the weapon still closer and deeper to my fluttering heart muscle. There is a popular tune in Northeastern Brazil that sings of the ruthlessness of these particular Brazilians of the state of Pernambuco —"*Sou Volente sou Pernanbucano!*"— Beware of me— I'm a Badddd-man from Pernambuco. I now had one on my ass and a mindless woman was driving him closer to killing...Me!

Iraci was so self consumed that she could not see the situation I had been thrust into. Well, I did what any right thinking man would or should do—apologized as profusely as I could in my suddenly now-tortured Portuguese, and with my other hand and mouth addressed the sweet banshee who had caused this very tense situation. And she kept giving this angry little man...my *coronel,* shit!

Even as I pressed my fingers over her jabbering jaws and told her to please shut the fuck up... She talked. But she did shut up though, because her jaws were clamped shut by my silent hand. Now she started to regain her wits as I kept on apologizing for the eternity it took for the elevator to jerk to a stop where I dragged Iraci out of the elevator and into the hall. The *coronel*, had business at a higher level, and without a hint of satisfaction on his face, put away his pistol and regained his position of authority as the elevator lurched up and away. Satisfaction is a big thing with *coronels.*

The rest of the trip to the consulate was anticlimactic. We found the stairs, climbed to the proper floor, found the office, got Iraci her papers and rode the elevator down, with me in control of fair damsel, yet all the while with the backwards glance in fear of seeing that little *coronel* with his shiny pistol in his crisp white suit. I took a cab to the airport for the flight to Rio and the dentist. Iraci in her flamboyant fashion, papers in hand, waved goodbye and returned to her apartment at the Hotel California with its thirteen floors of pleasure and pain.

That's the last I saw of Iraci, for sure, but seven years later I was in an upscale restaurant in Sausalito, California, where I maintained a studio. I thought she may have been among a group of noisy chattering ladies a few tables away. One sure looked like her and I strained to hear a Brazilian lilt to the English spoken, but I heard none. So I left well enough alone. I had come to recognize trouble with a capital T.

I often wonder if Iraci made it to her Denver. I hope she did. There must be some kind of reward to that kind of determination. As for the *coronel*, well, he taught me several important lessons "¡A *brincadeira e com outra!*" is certainly one lesson , and another is the dilemma of being linked to a loud-mouthed, crazed beauty. And of course to beware of a pint-sized, perfume dazzled coronel with a tiny, shiny *pistola* just inside his crisp white jacket.

Amerizil

The USA is a really strange place
I was born on the Fourth of July
I oughta know.
Being a White Black Man
or a Black White Man
and something of a student of History
I see America and Brazil morphing into one.
Amerizil
I Hope He Made It
He appeared out of nowhere
walking in the semi desert Sertao
of Northeastern Brazil
Edson —a strong black youth
with a burning future in his eyes.
"I am going to visit my cousin in Portland
State of Oregon in America
I do not have any money
I am going to walk there
I bet she will be surprised to see me:
'Edson has arrived
He has walked many thousands of kilometers
from Rio de Janeiro
to visit his cousin in America.'"
I hope he made it.

II

"I am going to leave this nigger hatin' America
and make it

I know I can make it
in Brazil."
She was black and beautiful and smart
ambition shining in her eyes
We had an art sale
a big art sale
She rented a house
invited the artists
invited the guests
(many with deep pockets)
and they came and danced
sipped champagne
drank wine
smoked joints
laughed and frolicked about
and bought paintings
and bought prints
and objects d' arte.
She made some money
and I know she left America
a couple of years later
I heard she made it to Rio
and I hope she made it.
Black folks suffered a lot
they hunger for a horizon
where the air is free and clear
and color-blind
I hope she made it
I hope they made it

I hope we all make it
helluvalot of obstructions
detours in the road, but
we can make it
I know we can make it.

1966—2011

LUNA
one helluva goat

Muffler Thoughts

Took the car for a new muffler
and had an hour to kill.
Around the corner and down the block
an auction house full of modern wonders and conveniences.
Lots of cars for sale
lots of cars and cars in lots
cars on the road
cars parked alongside the road.
Everywhere we turn there are cars,
trucks, and more cars.
I think back
40 years back
I was in a sleepy long forgotten town
in the Jaguaribe Valley in Northeastern Brazil.
It was Saturday, *Sabado*—Market day
Folks came in from the surrounding areas.
They came by horse
by burro (jumentos they call them)
and ox-drawn wooden semi-round-wheeled carts
Loaded with freshly fired pottery,
Recently slaughtered cows, pigs, goats
and other creatures
that look suspiciously like rats,
others that resemble domesticated critters.
A swish of a tail or tree branch wielded by a child
sends a dark hoard of flies
swirling, buzzing off the carcass momentarily.

From all directions
the campesinhos flood the market area
arriving hours before day-break
casting an eerie candle and lantern shadow.
Images fix on the mind
fixed in memory these past forty years
there they hang:
Cows' heads and pigs' heads in a row
suspended by the stretched tongue
nailed to the post above.
The eyes of the beast scream the last outrage
and the povo—the people
clamor for portions
their paltry earnings cannot afford.
By dawn most of the meat and eggs are gone
and the peasants—serfs really— are gathered
in noisy social groups
news, gossip and stories are exchanged—
cachaça—a devastating hard liquor is consumed
and poets on guitar
are the point of interest.
Laughter and frenzied shouts fill the air
as horse-traders make known
their phenomenal bargains.
The poor gather round
watching the traders show the hooves
bare the teeth and slap the flanks
exalting the genealogy of each and every beast.
It is one unmistakable continuity

of the human condition.
My head spins racing back through time
No tires are kicked
no horns are honked
The market is alive with sounds
Sounds that have been the voice of all mankind
for hundreds and thousands of years.
The smell, the sounds
The touch everyone's great-great-grandcestors knew.
But now my muffler is ready
and I'll be in my own tin can
alone with my thoughts:
Where am I going?
Where are we going?

Hawai'i and Brazil

Hawai'i and Brazil have many similarities in their economic and social evolution. There is also a curious look-alike to the political boundaries of Brazil and the Island of Hawai'i, where I have lived since 1973. It's as if Brazil had a baby and that baby is this tiny Island in the middle of the Pacific Ocean.

Furthermore, the Portuguese heritage, while being a dominant Western influence in Brazil, has also played a major role in the formation of modern Hawai'i, although rare indeed in the Islands are those who have maintained the language of their grandcestors. Plantation economics have formed both cultures, with workers from other regions of the world playing a dominant role in both contemporary societies. For better and for worse, tropical plants have been imported to the Islands, as have birds, insects and curious nuances in the language. We neither need nor want the snakes of the Amazon. Today, Brazil's economy is booming, and the "Sleeping Giant" has indeed awakened to take its rightful place among world leaders. It is a standing bit of tongue-in-cheek humor that Peace Corps Volunteers played a role in Brazil's successes since the end of the military dictatorship of the sixties and seventies. In truth PC Volunteers gained much more than they gave in the exchange, for we grew in self knowledge and global awareness. I continue to believe in people to people exchanges as the fundamental and essential link to forging a truly global community. The commonalities of different societies far outweigh their differences, and cultural difference makes for a richer world culture. It has been an honor to be a part of America's most noble experiment—I killed no one and made a helluva lot of friends. I'd like to believe that the foreign policy of all nations in the future will be based on people helping people across political and social frontiers—with Aloha— Hawai'i's unique and precious offering to the world.

Aloha 'Aina are magical words in the Hawaiian culture. The most common interpretation is "to love and care for the earth," but there is a deeper meaning that refers to an inner spirit of both the lover and the loved--the "Earth Spirit" as my Hawaiian elders teach. This, of course, is in keeping with indigenous peoples' religions and belief systems everywhere. All across the planet today, including, and especially Brazil, as we face ecological disaster, people are facing the reality that we must Aloha the 'Aina - care for and protect the Earth--Mother Earth, if we are to survive.

Manda Chuva (Rain Makers)

They held a grand party
in the fancy 'clube'
All the town was invited
and showed up
The poor were invited to watch us eat
We were invited
being Americanos and all
From behind wire fences they watched
tasting every bite of chicken with gravy
and chilled soda
even a beer
They were proud of the privileged of their town
The beggars laid low that evening
It was over early
One gets used to it
faces pressed into the wire fence
enjoying our supper for us
I remember mostly the children
What must they have thought
going home hungry?
Never mind saving the world
this was an anatomical dissection
of the world that is
The spiritual leaders were there
to comfort the rich
to comfort the poor
Everything will be alright
      bye and bye.

Padre Helio Campos (1911 - 1975)

was part of the great social upheaval that was generating in Brazil during the fifties and sixties. In 1962, with the combined efforts of the Catholic Church, unions, socialists, workers organizations, including the Communist Party of Brazil and a few well-to-do patriots, Padre Helio led a march of over 20,000 impoverished residents of Pirambú into the city center of Fortaleza, demanding relief from the inhuman living conditions in one of the worse favelas in all Brazil. The military coup of 1964 endangered all social reformists, the activist Catholic Church not excepted. Like Martin Luther King Jr., Padre Helio Campos is considered one of the great servants to humanity from within the Christian tradition.

One day as I sat with Padre Helio, which was rare, a young couple came up to him and asked to be married. She could not hide her obvious pregnancy. After they left, he smiled toward me and leaned back as if in great happiness at being Christ's servant, saying,

"As veces a chuva vem ante do tempo."

(Sometimes it rains before the rainy season.)

That's understanding human nature.

Made in the USA
Monee, IL
06 October 2023

43761617R00069